Canons and Connections

Canons and Connections

A Network Theory approach to the study of literary systems with specific reference to Afrikaans poetry

Burgert A. Senekal

Washington, DC

Copyright © 2014 by Burgert A. Senekal
New Academia Publishing 2014

All rights reserved. No part of this book may be reproduced or transmitted in any form or by any means, electronic or mechanical, including photocopying, recording, or by any information storage and retrieval system.

Printed in the United States of America

Library of Congress Control Number: 2014948032
ISBN 978-0-9904471-6-0   paperback (alk. paper)

New Academia Publishing
PO Box 27420, Washington, DC 20038-7420
info@newacademia.com - www.newacademia.com

Contents

Acknowledgements	ix
Preface	xi
A note on software	xvi
1. Introduction	1
2. From social networks to complex networks: A short history	11
3. Theoretical background	45
4. A macro level approach: The properties of complex networks	75
5. A micro level approach: Measures of centrality in the network	101
6. Centrality and marginality in the Afrikaans poetry network	111
7. Conclusion	129
Appendix A	133
Bibliography	137
Notes	149

To my father, Jan Senekal (1929-1995)

Acknowledgements

I would like to extend a special thanks to three people in particular. Firstly, Etienne van Heerden, the head of www.litnet.co.za, who encouraged me to do more and broader studies with this method. Secondly, Theo du Plessis, who offered me a position where I could devote my full attention to research. Thirdly, Dan Wasser, whose introduction to Sentinel Visualizer allowed me to explore networks further.

While this book is the result of research undertaken throughout 2011, 2012 and 2013, and necessarily incorporates the writings of theorists as well as insights gained throughout, the book is loosely based on two articles in particular (Senekal 2013a and 2013c), and it is hereby acknowledged that these articles were published in the journals *Stilet* and *Tydskrif vir Geesteswetenskappe* respectively.

Preface

I came to network theory by accident. In 2011, I received a research grant from the South African Heritage Foundation to study how information technology could be utilized in the study of Afrikaans literature, which gave me the impetus and financial resources to purchase and evaluate numerous software packages. I had realized that information overload was a major concern in an academic research context, and started out looking for software that would allow me to automate as much of the research process as possible; to eliminate all the 'donkey work,' which would allow me to spend more time reading, analyzing and writing. It soon became apparent that military intelligence was dealing with the same information overload I had encountered, and I started an enquiry on intelligence. This line of investigation soon led me to a program called Sentinel Visualizer, which is Social Network Analysis (SNA) software designed specifically for the US intelligence community. During the demonstration by Dan Wasser, Director of Business Development at FMS Advanced Systems Group, I realized that I had seen these concepts before: in polysystem theory. Perhaps that is where this story needs to start.

My father, J.H. (Jan) Senekal, was an academic and a professor in Afrikaans literature. He passed away in 1995, leaving his most prized books to me. At university, I had no intention of following in his footsteps, but one day, while browsing through the bookshelf in search of material to use for my Communication Science assignment, I picked up a book called *System and structure: Essays in communication and exchange* by Anthony Wilden (1980). The book intrigued me, and constituted my first contact with systems theory.

After completing my BA degree in 2001, I enrolled for a Master's degree in creative writing. Hereafter I enrolled for a Master's in English literature, which brought me back to Wilden. Wilden writes on alienation in terms of Lacan's *stade du mirroir*, and I believed alienation would be an interesting topic for a dissertation. In the end, alienation studies took me to Seeman (1959), and his modern interpreters. While doing research on the latter, I discovered Geyer (1996), whose focus on alienation within the framework of cybernetics led me back to Wilden. I read Wilden a couple of times cover to cover before I had a good understanding of what he was arguing – we had had no training in systems theory at university. In a chance meeting with Cristél Venter in London, I told her what I had been reading, and she suggested that I take a closer look at Ludwig von Bertalanffy (1968), whose name I recognized from Wilden. She also lent me her PhD-thesis (2002), in which I discovered Even-Zohar's polysystem theory (1979). By that time, my dissertation on alienation in contemporary British fiction was nearly finished, and I incorporated very little on systems theory.

Back in South Africa, I was appointed as a research assistant, where much of my work involved proofreading and translating articles before they were submitted to various journals. I soon wanted to publish my own article, and approached Margaret Raftery – one of my former supervisors – who suggested that I submit an article for her journal, *Textures*. Although not an accredited academic journal, she meticulously scrutinized everything submitted to *Textures*, which made it the perfect stepping-stone for an inexperienced young postgraduate. My first article, *The Mirror and the Universe in Christine Brooke-Rose's Life, End of*(2007), relied heavily on Wilden through a discussion of Lacan's mirror stage and non-equilibrium thermodynamics. This of course brought me even more in contact with the field of systems theory. The time soon came to start work on an accredited, mature article, and my first article utilized alienation theory: looking at how alienation is represented in a youth novel.

I remained with alienation theory until I received the grant from the Heritage Foundation. Why did I submit that application, and not for a project on alienation? I was convinced that I was not contributing much by looking at how alienation manifests in fiction, and thought there would be a better chance of obtaining funding if I submitted something that could offer results that are more tangible. I would expand my own knowledge and teach others to do research more efficiently, but for that, I needed funding to take financial risks on software that I eventually could have to discard. The Heritage Foundation provided this opportunity.

After my meeting with Dan Wasser, I started doing research on Social Network Analysis (SNA). About two months later, I had concluded that SNA could be used within the framework of polysystem theory, and I purchased the program (draining my remaining funding). I have always enjoyed exploring new terrains, and computer software is no different: I spent about a week or two experimenting, before getting a fair idea of how to operate my new analysis tool. At the time, my article on the project of the Heritage Foundation was already in the final stages (2012a), and my new SNA discovery was merely glanced over (with a few examples using Netdraw). However, an article on SNA followed a few weeks later, illustrating how we could use SNA to determine literary prestige (2012b).

My history with systems theory, networks, and complexity illustrates the roles that connections play. Although I had no idea that my father had worked within systems theory, and indeed that one of his publications (1987) is one of the seminal texts in terms of the Afrikaans literary system (along with those by Hein Viljoen), we did share one important connection: the bookshelf. Although I was too young at the time of his death to have discussed his ideas with him, he did therefore have a direct influence on my thinking, albeit through Wilden. Incidentally, Wilden is merely mentioned in a few passing references in Senekal (1987, 24, 45, 148, 172), illustrating what I would later learn to be the strength of weak ties, which is generally the best way to obtain new information.

Dan Wasser seemed skeptical when I told him what I wanted to do with Visualizer, but I persisted. Neither of us fully realized the potential that this partnership held: first looking at the Hertzog Literary Award (2013e), then the poetry network (2013a), then a citation analysis of academic publications (2014), and even studies on the Afrikaans film network, and now this book. SNA has allowed me to look at the Afrikaans cultural – not just literary – network on a much larger scale than I ever anticipated, and every new application brought new challenges and opportunities, as I came to know my software and theory better, as well as how this network functions. With ever-larger datasets, I also came to the conclusion that network theory offers not only a novel way of studying the literary system, but also one that draws on a vast corpus of publications on theory, which could also contribute to the study of a literary system on a theoretical level.

The academic community's reaction to my work has been mixed. Some of the feedback has been extremely positive, for instance, one reviewer wrote,

> It is innovative in terms of a fresh look at the Afrikaans poetry system. The article author should be congratulated that he/she approaches the Afrikaans literary field in an innovative way and thereby makes a contribution to the discussion on Afrikaans poetry.[1]

Others have been more skeptical; I quote another reviewer:

> A pigeon cooing 90 times in an oak lane will probably have a higher degree centrality than a lion roaring once in the same avenue. But who has the biggest impact / most influence? In the literary world, for example, it is well known that a publishing house such as Protea publishes the works of lesser poets, a fact which is also reflected in the limited number of prizes the writers who published at Protea earn. Yet, as indicated in the article, it is a fact that Protea published the most books of poetry. Books of poetry published at Protea are nevertheless on the periphery because of the inferior quality of the poetry.[2]

Both these reviews were in response to articles written on the Afrikaans poetry network. What the second reviewer did not understand is that degree centrality alone does not guarantee a position at the center of the network, and degree centrality is certainly not a measure of influence (although, in contrast with the reviewer's claims, many of the most prestigious Afrikaans poets do publish through Protea, such as Joan Hambidge, Marius Crous, Lina Spies,

George Weideman, Daniel Hugo, and Hennie Aucamp). Part of the problem that can be seen from the second reviewer's comment, therefore, is that there is no real understanding of where network theory fits in with the existing polysystem- and field theories that have been used in literary studies for decades, and how. This is one of the main objectives of this book: To discuss the theory and applications in more detail than I have had space for in articles, and thereby limit future misunderstandings.

With every mini project of mine, I have read more and more on network theory, becoming ever more enthusiastic. Steven Strogatz (2004[2003], 232) seems to share my enthusiasm, "If the day should ever come that we understand how life emerges from a dance of lifeless chemicals, or how consciousness arises from billions of unconscious neurons, that understanding will surely rest on a deep theory of complex networks." I agree, but I will leave him and his colleagues to refine the theory. In the meantime, applying network theory to ever more diverse, comprehensive and unexplored datasets keeps me constantly exploring.

Burgert A. Senekal
University of the Free State
2014

A note on software

While Pajek and UCINET are the most popular SNA programs in the academic community, there are literally hundreds of software platforms available. No doubt, some are better than others are, while the majority is similarly effective. My choice of Sentinel Visualizer was based on two issues in particular: Firstly, I found Visualizer easier to work with. I work with many different kinds of networks, and have worked on right-wing extremists, bank directors, poets and artists, film actors and other industry role players, and citations. Every network has different entity[3] types, and being able to adapt quickly is important in my work. Visualizer allowed me to customize entity and relationship types quickly and effectively, and go from data preparation to a preliminary analysis without wasting time.

Secondly, Visualizer allowed me to export an entity list to Microsoft Excel, which made it easier to ensure that the same entities are not read as more than one entity. Sometimes even an extra space in an Excel spreadsheet would create an extra entity in the database, or an author would be referred to by one initial in one text, two initials in another, and by his full name in a third. This naming inconsistency of source documents results in one author actually becoming three or more, and the researcher needs to find a way of making sure that his network only considers one person in this instance. Visualizer allowed me to ensure, efficiently and accurately, that my network data is correct.

There are other programs that also satisfy these criteria, but Visualizer's intuitive import procedure and analysis options work well for me.

That said, Visualizer has its shortcomings. Visualizer cannot calculate average path length, average clustering, and other complex network features that are usually associated with a macro-level approach. However, I believe it is better in my case not to spend too much time on measuring the poetry network against other complex networks, for it has been proven in numerous studies that complex networks exhibit highly similar structural characteristics (such as small-worldedness). Proving that the Afrikaans poetry network exhibits the same structural characteristics does not say much about the Afrikaans poetry network itself, nor does it, in my view, contribute much to our general understanding of complex networks. The development and refining of the theory of complex networks is in my view better left to physicists such as Duncan Watts, Mark Newman, Steven Strogatz, and Albert-Lazló Barabási – it is not my objective to contribute to the theory, but rather to use the theory to contribute to our understanding of the literary network. Therefore, Visualizer's shortcomings will only affect a study that measures the poetry network against other complex networks; for using the theory to come to a better understanding of the poetry network, Visualizer is, in my view, ideal. That said, I use Gephi for the visualization of various example networks where macrolevel topological features are discussed, because Gephi is better suited to this level of analysis.

Ultimately, the use of a computer program should depend not on what is most popular, but on which program serves the researcher best in answering his questions in a scientifically valid and methodologically sound manner. Although other researchers may feel that their software platforms are superior, I believe Visualizer serves my purpose best.

1

Introduction

> Today we increasingly recognize that nothing happens in isolation. Most events and phenomena are connected, caused by, and interacting with a huge number of other pieces of a complex universal puzzle. We have come to see that we live in a small world, where everything is linked to everything else. We are witnessing a revolution in the making as scientists from all different disciplines discover that complexity has a strict architecture. We have come to grasp the importance of networks. *Albert-Lazló Barabási* (2003[2002], 7)

Over the past two decades, the scientific community has increasingly focused on issues relating to connectedness – Duncan Watts (2004[2003], 14) even refers to the contemporary period as the "Connected Age." Through the Internet and social media such as Facebook, Twitter, and YouTube, the world has indeed become a smaller place, and how people and concepts are related has become a topic of popular discussion. Of course, the issue of connectedness was highlighted by the famed Kevin Bacon game, as well as the "Six degrees of Monica Lewinsky," but also global epidemics such as SARS and the H5N1 virus has brought home the fact that the world has become smaller, which has both positive and negative consequences.

Much of this connectedness is the result of technology, in terms of both transport and the Internet, while some has been political. The end of the Cold War – and the near-simultaneous end to apartheid – has opened up borders, in particular for South Africans. While many members of family or old friends used the economic and political opportunities to disperse, Facebook, email, and Skype has made it possible to keep in touch. I remember how exited my father was when he started using email in the early 1990s; we had no idea that fifteen years later I would be holding a video conference via Skype with friends from all over the globe on a Friday night instead of going out.

The interest in complex systems and networks is one of the symptoms of this increasing connectedness; as Steven Strogatz (2004[2003], 230) proposes, "[S]cience itself reflects the network zeitgeist." Costa et al. (2011, 331) also note a general trend in science towards integrationist approaches, and an interest in studying nonlinear phenomena. Systems theory – and network theory – has existed in some form or another from the eighteenth century, but its earlier adoption was much slower than in recent years. Particularly in sociology and physics, network theory and the study of complexity has gained ground since the late 1990s, and when Mayer-Schönberger and Cukier (2013) discuss the uses of Big Data and the possible scientific revolution this entails, the network theorists are again in the spotlight. Borgatti et al. (2009, 892) contend, "Network research is 'hot' today, with the number of articles in the Web of Science on the topic of 'social networks' nearly tripling in the past

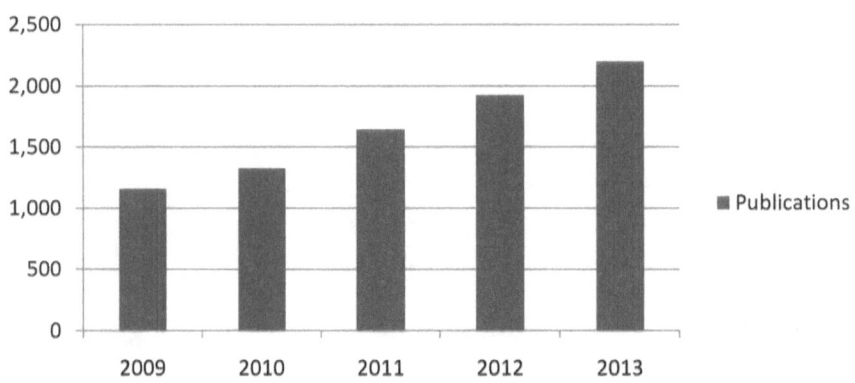

Publications on [social networks] over the past 5 years

decade." A search done on 5 May 2014 on Thompson Scientific's *Web of Science* with the term [social networks],[4] shows that 9,882 studies have been published (according to this database) over the past 5 years. In addition, the number of studies published each year has shown a steady increase:

Besides physics and sociology, fields such as economics have also embraced network theory, where of course the interactions between people, companies and countries has often led to unpredictable and complex interactions. Smith and White (1992, 861) remark that Snyder and Kick (1979) and Steiber (1979) were "the first explicit attempts to use the network approach to examine the world-system," and since them global economic systems have been approached as networks in numerous studies (see Nemeth and Smith 1985, Smith and White 1992, De Benedictis and Tajoli 2008, and Flandreau and Jobst 2005, 2009). Fricke, Finger, and Lux (2013, 2) write,

> [I]nvestigations of complex systems in terms of their network properties gain more and more attention in economics following the lead of other disciplines in which network analyses have already a long tradition.

The study of language as a system has been a common practice since De Saussure's seminal publication. In Saussure's (1966, 114) definition, language "is a system of interdependent terms in which the value of each term results solely from the simultaneous presence of the others." More recently, language has been studied as a *complex* system (see e.g. Weideman 2011 and Kwapień and Drożdż 2012, 129), and more importantly, as a *complex network*. In such a linguistic network, the links between lexical items may be as simple as co-occurrences, or they may be semantic (synonyms, hyponyms, antonyms etc.) (see Solé et al. (2010), and Dorogovtsev and Mendes (2001).

Literary studies may have been slow to share the enthusiasm shown by these scientific fields in the study of complexity, but a literary variant of systems theory – polysystem theory – has (formally) existed since Itamar Even-Zohar's (1979) seminal publication. Van Gorp (1997, 1) notes that "systemic" terms can already be found in the works of Jurij Tynjanov and Jurij Lotman, Claudio Guillén and Robert Estival, but it was only since the 1970s that Niklas Luhmann, Siegfried J. Schmidt, and Even-Zohar institutionalized this approach. Even-Zohar based his hypothesis on writers considered to belong to the Russian Formalist movement, and this hypothesis was subsequently expanded into a theory by members of the Porter Institute for Poetics and Semiotics at the University of Tel Aviv, in particular Gideon Toury, Zohar Shavit, and Rakefet Sheffy (Codde 2003, 91). The field theory of the French sociologist Pierre Bourdieu is often integrated with polysystem theory, and Codde writes that Even-Zohar often uses Bourdieu's concept of *habitus* as if polysystem theory's views on cultural systems and field theory's views are interchangeable.[5] Both field theory and polysystem theory (and a combination thereof) have been shown to offer valuable insights in the study of cultural systems, as the many works by Dirk de Geest, Kees van Rees, Elrud Ibsch, Gillis Dorleijn, Douwe Fokkema and others show (see Van Rees and Dorleijn 2006 and Venter 2006, 35-36). In 1987, Senekal (1987, 22) wrote, "Nowadays, literature is widely viewed as a system, and not as a collection of books/text/linguistic constructs."[6] Ten years later, Schmidt (1997, 119) claimed, "no literary scholar who wants to be taken seriously by the academic world would deny that it is inadequate to study literary texts in isolation from their contexts."

Since it was introduced in South Africa in the mid-1980s, numerous studies have used polysystem theory to study the interactions between entities in the Afrikaans literary system. The first studies were those by Hein Viljoen, Jan Senekal, and the SENSAL project, and subsequently Bernard Odendaal and Hennie van Coller, as well as their students, have kept this approach alive in Afrikaans literature, along with scholars such as Francis Galloway and Rudi Venter (see Viljoen 1984, Viljoen 1986, Senekal 1986, Senekal 1987, John 1994, Van Coller 2002, Venter 2002, Van Coller and Odendaal 2003, Greyling 2005, Venter 2006, Van Coller and Odendaal 2008, and Van Coller 2011). Polysystem theory has become so ingrained in Afrikaans literary studies that it no longer warrants a detailed theoretical treatment in academic articles: most authors are content with a passing reference to Even-Zohar, as the theory is now 'business as usual.'

Despite literary studies' familiarity with the concepts of systems theory, the study of literary systems has however not kept pace with developments in other fields that deal with complex systemic relations. Since the mid-1990s, complex systems theory has gained prominence in other scientific fields, and with it, network theory. In physics, Amaral and Ottino (2004, 147) argue, "Network theory is now an essential ingredient in the study of complex systems," and Maslov, Sneppen, and Zaliznyak (2004, 529) note, "Networks have emerged as a unifying theme in complex systems research." Yet complex networks remain a largely undeveloped field in literary studies. Wouter de Nooy (1991, 1993, 2002) – who integrates SNA with Bourdieu's field theory[7]– is a notable exception, and in South Africa, Senekal (2012b and 2013c) has suggested that it could be a useful approach to literary systems. Nevertheless, this approach remains largely unknown within the study of literature.

Network theory offers a valuable way of making the study of literary systems – and cultural fields in general –a more objective undertaking. Polysystem theory did not change the way literary studies are conducted, and Van Coller (2011, 69) for instance writes, "The inherent lack of systems thinking is the impossibility of verification because it is an interpretive construction."[8] The usual way polysystem theory is applied in Afrikaans literary studies is to use the theory as a starting point from where relationships are merely described, which turns the theory into a proverbial coat rack on which to hang a description. For example, Van Coller (2011) gives a short description of an aspect of the functioning of open systems (the conflict between core and periphery), after which he starts a description of the relationship between middlebrow and canonized literature. In this study – which is exemplary of the application of polysystem theory in Afrikaans literary studies – the theoretical background serves only to inform the coming description of literary debates and novels.

Network analysis however offers a way to *illustrate* how prestige is accumulated through the interactions between role players within the literary system, as well as providing a way to *prove* that the literary system is indeed a complex system. Already in 1987, Jan Senekal (1987, 24) called for a more scientific study of literature,

> A literary studies which analyses the literary system/systems, and which does not claim for itself a 'special status and otherness', which is not directed by poetics and attitudes but by scientific-philosophical considerations, can examine what a system looks like, how it functions, or whether the community is satisfied with it. Furthermore, it can describe the internal relations between literary production, literary distribution, literary reception and literary processing or consumption.[9]

Network theory has the potential to approach literary systems differently: not by being a new theory, but rather a new approach within an existing theory, and a more objective one at that. The quoted reviewer's report (see Preface) referred to the 'quality' of poetry, which is a subjective judgment, and the reviewer took exception that what he deemed of low quality was considered part of the core of the network. Network theory is not concerned with such subjective judgments; it asks what the network looks like, and how it functions, as Jan Senekal called for.

In addition, as Haythomthwaite (1996, 325) acknowledges, "Social network analysis strives to derive social structure empirically, based on observed relationships between actors, rather than on a priori classifications." Network theory is for instance not concerned with who the most important literary publisher *should* be, or the most influential critic; it analyzes the actual roles entities fulfill within the structure of the network. This ability of SNA promises to challenge assumptions, and it has already been shown that the perceived "important" journals of Afrikaans literary scholarship in South Africa are not necessarily the most cited (B. A. Senekal 2014).

One of the advantages of network theory that appealed to me from the start has been its ability to model the system through a visual representation (a *graph* or *sociogram*). For thirty years, scholars in Afrikaans literary studies have been referring to the literary system, but it was always something abstract; intangible. Network visualizations make the system concrete: something we, as well as our students, can more easily comprehend.

A last advantage of network theory that cannot be overstated is its interdisciplinary applications. Indeed, Freeman (2004, 5) writes that SNA is *characterized* by its wide range of applications. Costa et al. (2011, 331) argue, "The success of complex networks is [...] to a large extent a consequence of their natural suitability to represent virtually any discrete system," and Barabási (2009, 413) also notes the variety of subjects that can be studied with this approach,

> Today the understanding of networks is a common goal of an unprecedented array of traditional disciplines: Cell biologists use networks to make sense of signal transduction cascades and metabolism, to name a few applications in this area; computer scientists are mapping the Internet and the WWW; epidemiologists follow transmission networks through which viruses spread; and brain researchers are after the connectome, a neural-level connectivity map of the brain. Although many fads have come and gone in complexity, one thing is increasingly clear: Interconnectivity is so fundamental to the behavior of complex systems that networks are here to stay.

The interdisciplinary applications of network theory have important consequences for the study of the literary system. As will be shown later in this book, the Matthew Effect (preferential attachment), degree correlation and other concepts developed in the theory of complex networks have an important bearing on our understanding of how literary systems function. Duncan Watts's experiments (see e.g. Watts and Hasker 2006) with music choices have already provided a suggestion as to how popularity accrues, which may provide new insights into how literary fame is developed and maintained. In general, network theory offers many robust scientific concepts with which to analyze literary systems; the suggestion made in this book is that these could be used to better our understanding of the object of our scientific interest as well.

Because network theory is interdisciplinary, discoveries made in a field that would usually be regarded as far from literary studies, e.g. microbiology, can have an impact on how we view the functioning of the system. The cross-pollination of concepts is perhaps the greatest promise network theory holds, for it allows the study of Afrikaans literature – which is minute compared to other scientific fields – to draw on vast experience and a global scientific community's findings and insights. Using these insights from other scientific fields not only breaks down barriers between disciplines, but also can lead to new – and scientifically well-grounded – insights about our field.

Following Senekal (2013c, 2013a, 2012b), this book analyses the Afrikaans poetry system from 2000 to 2012 within the framework of network theory, arguing that by approaching the literary system as a network, the possibility opens up to utilize methods, theoretical insights and software that allow a more scientific modeling of the system. For this study, a list of books of poetry published since 2000, as compiled by Marlise Joubert and available at www.versindaba.co.za, was analyzed. A database was compiled, which records details regarding these publications, as well as their links with other stakeholders. Joubert was also kind enough to post links to reviews, but since she does not claim that her list is complete, further searches had to be done using the profiles of authors www.litnet.co.za (as largely compiled by Erika Terblanche), and thereafter more searches were done on Sabinet's *ePublications* database and various search engines to ensure that the data is as comprehensive as possible, taking into account reviews in newspapers, magazines, academic journals and on websites. This information was then entered into the database, in other words, *who* reviewed *which* volume of poetry, and *where* the review appeared. Academic studies were also found using searches on Sabinet's *ePublications* database as well as searches on search engines, in order to include further studies of poets' works in the database, including academic articles and MA dissertations and PhD theses. Again, the publishing platform, as well as the author of the study, was noted. Although I do not want to claim that this data set is entirely complete, an attempt was made to ensure that the data set is as comprehensive as possible, and this data set is more comprehensive than the ones available on www.versindaba.co.za or www.litnet.co.za, or both: additional searches often led to further discoveries. In total, there are 278 books of poetry in this network, along with 1071 reviews, interviews, and studies.

Note however that no distinction was made here by the researcher between books belonging to elite (highbrow) literature

(literature proper), and popular (lowbrow) literature. Jan Senekal (1987, 185) writes,

> When literature is not construed as the small number of books and authors on the E-plane, but as acts in a literary communication system that covers the entire range, one can get a more complete picture of how the literary system is compiled and organized. This is what we are concerned with here.[10]

In following Jan Senekal, this study is not only concerned with highbrow – all poetry books have been considered, regardless of whether they were judged to be 'good' or 'bad', because all publications contribute to the literary system in their own way. At the very least, a poets' works cannot be central to the network if there is no periphery, and so *every* publication ultimately influences the functioning of the system. In addition, selecting only works that are considered 'worthy' of study is scientifically unsound in itself: judging 'quality' is best left to the critics.

2

From social networks to complex networks: A short history

Network theory's interdisciplinary applications are mirrored by its diverse roots, ranging from the purely mathematical to the sociological and anthropological. Although a more detailed overview of network theory's development can for instance be found in Freeman (2004), Amaral and Ottino (2004), and Prell (2012), the current chapter provides an historical overview of how this interdisciplinary field evolved in order to contextualize some of network theory's theoretical developments that will be discussed later in the book.

Network theory is closely intertwined with graph theory, a branch of mathematics, which also constitutes network theory's oldest foundation. The development of graph theory is usually traced to Leonard Euler's famous Königsberg bridge puzzle, as formulated in 1736 (Hu 2011, 180 and Boccaletti et al. 2006, 177). Euler writes,

> In the town of Königsberg in Prussia there is an island A, called 'Kneiphoff', with the two branches of the river (Pregel) flowing around it. There are seven bridges, a, b, c, d, e, f, and g, crossing the two branches. The question is whether a person can plan a walk in such a way that he will cross each of these bridges once but not more than once. [...] On the basis of the above I formulated the following very general problem for myself: Given any configuration of the river and the branches into which it may divide, as well as any number of bridges, to determine whether or not it is possible to cross each bridge exactly once.[11]

12   *Canons and Connections*

Euler demonstrated that the puzzle could not be solved – there was no way in which all bridges could be crossed only once. In the process, however, he illustrated that physical distance had no relation to his puzzle, and was therefore the first to represent a network as a graph:

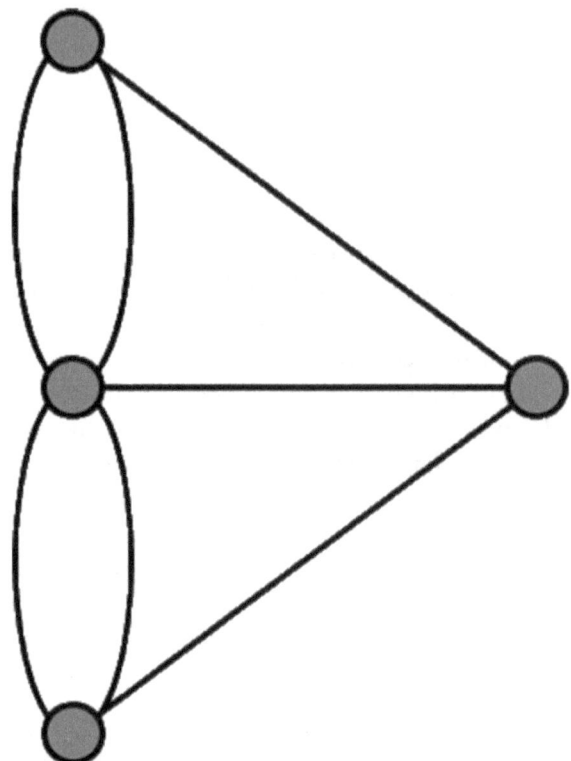

Euler's Königsberg bridge puzzle

In the above graph, the bridges are represented as links connecting nodes, which represent the different margins and islands.

Jacob Moreno's (and Helen Jennings's[12]) *Who shall survive?* (1934) was "a signal event in the history of social network analysis" (Freeman 2004, 7). Moreno and Jennings investigated why 14 girls from the Hudson School for Girls in New York had run away in just two weeks, and suggested that the phenomenon had less to do with the girls' intrinsic characteristics and more to do with their positions in a social network. Moreno used a technique he called "sociometry," which graphically represented the social network in what Moreno called a *sociogram*. Moreno (1934, 11) wrote that this approach, "enquire[s] into the evolution and organization of groups and the position of individuals within them." Similar to Euler's Königsberg bridge puzzle, Moreno emphasized structure over physical distance, where social influence would spread along connections between the girls.

Moreno's conception of social networks influencing individual behavior was of course not an isolated view, for throughout the twentieth century, numerous sociologists adopted a systems-theoretical perspective on societies. Emile Durkheim for instance argued that societies were comparable to biological systems, consisting of interrelated components, thus emphasizing the structure of the system over the intrinsic characteristics of its components. Borgatti et al. (2009, 892) write, "Moreno's sociometry provided a way of making this abstract social structure tangible." Sociometry is widely regarded as a forerunner of SNA, but Freeman (1996, 2004) notes that the roots of SNA are complex, and could also be traced to the works of among others Almack (1922), Wellman (1926), Chevaleva-Janovskaja (1927), Bott (1928), Hubbard (1929), and Hagman (1933).

Another clear antecedent of SNA was the works of Kurt Lewin. Lewin saw the social environment as a "field" (like the later Bourdieu[13]), which he defined as, "the totality of coexisting facts which are conceived of as mutually interdependent" (Lewin 1951, 240). Lewin (1939, 889) writes,

> Whether or not a certain type of behavior occurs depends not on the presence or absence of one fact or of a number of facts as viewed in isolation but upon the constellation (structure and forces) of the specific field as a whole. The 'meaning' of the single fact depends upon its position in the field; or, to say the same in more dynamical terms, the different parts of a field are mutually interdependent.

In terms of the social field, Lewin came to a similar conclusion as Euler had when attempting to solve the Königsberg puzzle, "the social field is actually an empirical space, which is as 'real' as a physical one. Euclidean space generally is not suited for adequately representing the structure of a social field – for instance, the relative position of groups, or a social locomotion" (Lewin 1939, 891). Like Moreno, then, Lewin applied a similar logic to social systems as Euler had done in his puzzle, further cementing the graphical representation of social systems as networks. Lewin also introduced the concept of the "shortest path" to sociology (Bavelas 1948, 17).

In these beginning years, SNA's roots branch out across various disciplines (e.g. graph theory and sociology). Another discipline that would eventually have an important influence on the emerging science of networks was anthropology. Borgatti et al. (2009, 893) write,

> ... building on the insights of the anthropologist Levi-Strauss, scholars began to represent kinship systems as relational algebras that consisted of a small set of generating relations (such as "parent of" and "married to") together with binary composition operations to construct derived relations such as "in-law" and "cousin." It was soon discovered that the kinship systems of such peoples as the Arunda of Australia formed elegant mathematical structures that gave hope to the idea that deep lawlike regularities might underlie the apparent chaos of human social systems.

The anthropologist Alex Bavelas (1948) was a student of Kurt Lewin, and introduced the concept of centrality in social networks. Although he set out to define what Freeman (1977) later formalized as betweenness centrality,[14] the measure he developed was nearer to closeness centrality, which measures not control over information in a network but rather independence of control (1980, 585, 593). Nevertheless, Freeman credits Bavelas for his "intuition" that contributed to the future important development of both betweenness and closeness centralities, which are discussed later in this book.

Kochen and Pool's studies in the 1950s led them to the definition of random graphs (Amaral and Ottino 2004, 152) and the identification of what is known today as the small-world phenomenon. Borgatti et al. (2009, 892) write, "On the basis of mathematical models, they speculated that in a population like the United States, at least 50% of pairs could be linked by chains with no more than two intermediaries." Although their work was only published towards the late 1970s (see e.g. Pool and Kochen 1979), it was widely circulated in preprint form, and is regarded as a direct influence on Stanley Milgram's "six degrees of separation" (1967) studies (Amaral and Ottino 2004, 152).

Like Kurt Lewin and Emile Durkheim, Siegfried Frederick Nadel (1957) saw societies not as monolithic entities, but rather as a "pattern or network (or 'system') of relationships obtaining between actors in their capacity of playing roles relative to one another" (Nadel 1957, 12). Nadel's work was one of the earliest formal treatments of the subject, and directly influenced the later work of Harrison White (Prell 2012, 34).

In the 1960s, the center of gravity of network research shifted from anthropology to sociology (Borgatti, Mehra, et al. 2009, 893). One of the foremost social network theorists was Linton Freeman, who formalized betweenness, closeness and degree centrality, with all three forms of centrality placing different emphasis on what happens in a network (see Freeman 1977, 1979, 1980). However, it was only in the late 1960s and 1970s that SNA developed into a separate field within sociology, especially at Harvard, where Harrison White institutionalized SNA.[15] White worked with many other influential researchers, including Stanley Milgram, and Mark Granovetter was one of his students. Granovetter (1973) studied the links that connect different clusters in a network, and proposed that 'weak ties' have special importance in spreading information in social networks – a key concept in contemporary network theory. Barry Wellman, another former student of White, would later form the International Network Society of Social Network Analysts (INSNA) (http://www.insna.org/), which publishes amongst others the journal *Connections*. Borgatti et al. (2006, 893) write that by the 1980s, "social network analysis had become an established field within the social sciences, with a professional organization (INSNA), an annual conference (Sunbelt), specialized software (e.g., UCINET), and its own journal (*Social Networks*)."

Within mathematics, one of the most influential advancements of graph theory was developed by Paul Erdös and Alfréd Rényi (1960). Their model laid the foundation for network models that would later develop into the scale-free and small-world models (see below).

In the late 1990s, networks became an object of interest from physicists. The first seminal publication was a paper by Duncan Watts and Steven Strogatz (1998), which appeared in *Nature* and argued that the small-world property of networks – as proposed by Stanley Milgram (1967) – was a universal attribute of complex networks, and not just of social networks. In other words, power grids, metabolic processes, neural networks, and other kinds of complex networks were comparable with social networks in terms of the average number of links that needed to be traversed to reach a node from any other node. Albert and Barabási (2002, 68) write that this paper caused an "avalanche of research on the properties of small-world networks," particularly in the physics community. Network analysis was now more than just SNA: it had become an instrument in the study of complexity in general, as Strogatz (2004[2003], 232) writes, "the 'small-world' phenomenon is much more than a curiosity of human social life: It's a unifying feature of diverse networks found in nature and technology."

In 1999, Barabási and Albert (1999) published an article in *Science* that argued that complex networks are scale-free networks that adhere to the so-called power law, which is discussed later. Boccaletti et al. (2006, 177) write that these two papers in particular "triggered" a "flurry of activity" in the physics community, directly leading to the popularity of this approach. The natural sciences in particular have focused their attentions on developing and refining models to come to a better understanding of complexity in networks. By 2004, Strogatz (2004[2003], 256) writes,

> In the past five years, the new ideas of small-world and scale-free networks have triggered an explosion of empirical studies dissecting the structure of complex networks. In case after disparate case, when the flesh is peeled back, the same skeletal structure appears from within. The Internet backbone and the primate brain – both small worlds. So are the food webs of species preying on each other, the meshwork of metabolic reactions in the cell, the interlocking boards of directors of the Fortune 1,000 companies, even the structure of the English language itself.

Along with these developments, growing computer power and the availability of large digital datasets had a profound influence on the development of the field (see Freeman 2004, 139, Barabási 2009, 413, Watts 2011, 82, and Scott 2012, 6). Network theory is heavily dependent upon computer-generated analyses, as already argued by Boissevain (1979, 392), and the development of cheaper, more user-friendly and more widely available software and hardware empowered a larger group of scientists to study networks. In the 1970s, programs such as DIP, SocPac, SOCK, COMPLT, BLOCKER and CONCOR (see Tichy, Tushman and Fombrun 1979, 513) facilitated network analysis, while by the 1990s, GRADAP, STRUCTURE, UCINET, NEGOPY and KRACKPLOT were used extensively (Haythomthwaite 1996, 331). Currently, Pajek is one of the most popular programs, along with UCINET, but a wide variety of network analysis programs have been developed – even a non-academic application to analyze Facebook contacts (TouchGraph). Anyone can now use SNA to look at his friends' connections on Facebook: SNA is no longer an approach limited to computer-savvy academics, but a tool with popular appeal outside academia.

The World Wide Web also allowed the gathering of larger datasets, which is one of the main reasons Watts and Strogatz could undertake their landmark study of small-worldedness in complex networks. Albert and Barabási (2002, 483) recognize this availability of digital data in their overview of the factors that contributed to the popularity of network theory,

> First, the computerization of data acquisition in all fields led to the emergence of large databases on the topology of various real networks. Second, the increased computing power allowed us to investigate networks containing millions of nodes, exploring questions that could not be addressed before. Third, the slow but noticeable breakdown of boundaries between disciplines offered researchers access to diverse databases, allowing them to uncover the generic properties of complex networks. Finally, there is an increasingly voiced need to move beyond reductionist approaches and try to understand the behavior of the system as a whole.

Dempwolf and Lyles (2012, 4) remind us that SNA is *both* a theoretical perspective *and* a practical set of analytical tools, as the above example of TouchGraph illustrates. The last major benefactor of network theory was the tremendous financial injection awarded to the development of software applications for SNA from a military intelligence standpoint. Unlike during the Cold War, where the US had faced a mostly monolithic enemy with a hierarchical organization and power base susceptible to attack, Al-Qaeda and its affiliates were an entirely different enemy altogether. Although Al-Qaeda had (at the time) a leadership hierarchy, small cells were capable of operating virtually independently, supplied through vast, global financial networks. Transnational terrorist networks, the Intelligence Community (IC) recognized, had to be approached *as a network,* and for that, they needed the tools to find the ties between members of terrorist organizations.[16] Already in the early 1990s, Sparrow (1991) advocated for the application of network analysis to criminal intelligence, and Glenn Henke (2009, 5) calls Arquilla, Ronfeldt and Zanini's (1999) RAND report on *Networks, Netwar, and Information-Age Terrorism,* "the first dedicated analysis of information age terrorism." Soon after the invasion of Afghanistan, studies using SNA to map terrorist networks emerged. Valdis Krebs (2002) was the first to publish a study using SNA to investigate terrorist networks, where he used open-source information to map the ties between the 9/11 hijackers, indicating that Mohamed Atta was the ring leader (Krebs 2002, 47) by using Freeman's (1979) formulas for betweenness-, closeness- and degree centralities. Rodriguez (2005) mapped the network responsible for the March 2004 Madrid bombings, Carley et al. (2003) analyzed the Al-Qaeda cell that was responsible for the bombing in Tunisia, while Koschade (2006) mapped Jemaah Islamiyah. In 2005, the Committee on Network Science for Future Army Applications (2005) published a special report on the utility of network theory. David Petraeus (2006) also includes a special section on SNA for military intelligence purposes in the new *US Army and Marine Corps Counterinsurgency Field Manual.* Numerous software platforms, including Sentinel Visualizer, Starlight VIS, and i2 Analyst's Notebook were developed from increased defense expenditure. Ressler (2006, 7) notes that government agencies, such as the Defense Advanced Research Projects

Agency (DARPA), the National Security Agency (NSA), and the Department of Homeland Security (DHS), have funded research related to SNA. Borgatti et al. (2009, 893) write that people working within security utilized SNA extensively,

> Of all the applied fields, national security is probably the area that has most embraced social network analysis. Crime-fighters, particularly those fighting organized crime, have used a network perspective for many years, covering walls with huge maps showing links between 'persons of interest.' This network approach is often credited with contributing to the capture of Saddam Hussein. In addition, terrorist groups are widely seen as networks rather than organizations, fueling research on how to disrupt functioning networks. At the same time, it is often asserted that it takes a network to fight a network, sparking military experiments with decentralized units.

The application of SNA for intelligence purposes is however not the only practical application of this approach. Zhu, Watts, and Chen (2010, 151) write,

> ...firms are using social network analysis to make hiring and transfer decisions, to optimize the flow of information among their employees, and to get the most out of talent and ideas that are embedded in the social networks of their staff.

Network theory's wide academic applications sets it apart from most other scientific theories, for it is truly interdisciplinary. However, these practical applications within military intelligence and business also sets it apart from other theoretical approaches in another way: it has been applied in the non-academic world, and found useful. Network theory's utility has therefore been demonstrated not only across academic disciplines, but also in practice, which is a relatively unique feature of the theory of complex networks as compared with other theories.

3

Theoretical background

Introduction

Culture is a web, not a piece of printing in isolation – Jan Senekal (1987, 44)[17]

Systems theory evolved in different guises throughout the 20th century, often called by different terms, e.g. General Systems Theory (Von Bertalanffy 1968), Complex Adaptive Systems or CAS (see e.g. Amaral and Ottino 2004 and Heylighen 2007), and Dynamic Systems (see e.g. Bar-Yam 1997), and is closely related to cybernetics,[18] and non-equilibrium thermodynamics (see Von Bertalanffy 1968, Wilden 1980 and Prigogine 1997). Polysystem theory, which is based primarily on the works of the Russian Formalists, shares concepts with systems theory in general, whether called Complex Adaptive Systems, complex systems, or General Systems after Von Bertalanffy. The theoretical developments in the study of complex systems in the 1990s contributed further concepts and understanding of mankind's environment, all of which necessitates a general discussion of systems *as systems* here (as opposed to the next chapter, where systems are discussed *as networks*).

Von Bertalanffy (1968, 55) defines a system as "a set of elements standing in interrelations." The key term in this definition is "interrelations:" Kwapień and Drożdż (2012, 205) write, "The most fundamental factor that shapes complex systems are the interactions among their elements" (see also Senekal 1987, 172). Collections of entities that are not related in a meaningful way do not comprise a system. For instance, a pistol is composed of numerous interrelated parts: a barrel, spring, slide, magazine, etcetera, that accomplish a greater function than the individual parts would have been able to accomplish on their own: firing a bullet. A pistol can therefore be called a system, because its component parts are *interrelated*. On the other hand, a box of bullets is not interrelated: it remains a collection of single elements that are not capable of achieving any further functionality than the individual parts are each capable of.

To illustrate the concept of relatedness, Miller and Page (2007, 45) use the example of a picture composed of mosaic tiles, which is adapted here. Consider the following picture:

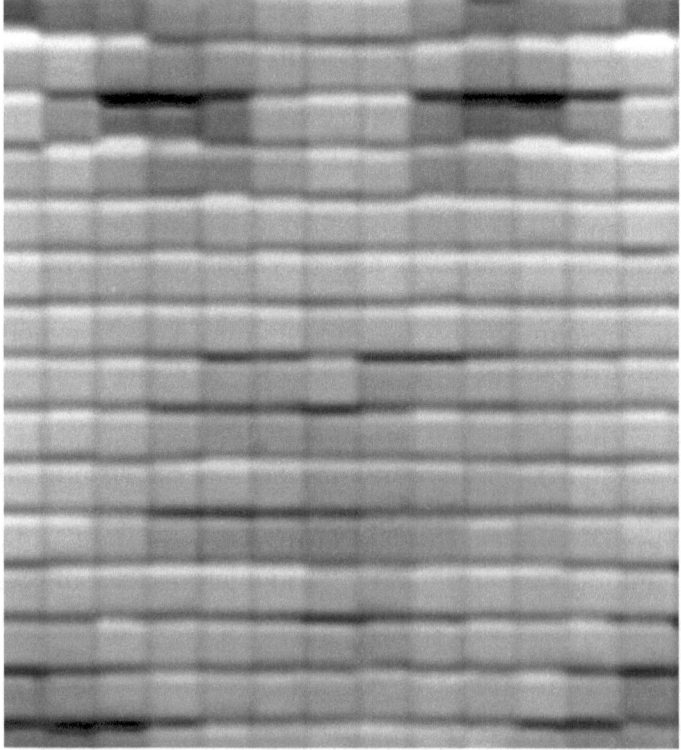

Interrelatedness Part1

These tiles offer a range of colors, but the way in which they are arranged suggests that these are not simply random tiles: by zooming out, it can be seen that they clearly represent a face:

Theoretical background 23

Interrelatedness Part 2

While each individual tile does not form a picture in itself, their combination results in a recognizable picture of a human being. This characteristic of systems is usually called *emergence*, which is "a spontaneous occurrence of macroscopic order from a sea of randomly interacting elements on a microscopic level" (Kwapień and Drożdż 2012, 118, see also Miller and Page 2007, 44 and Midgley 2000, 40). Emergence is the term that captures the familiar statement that 'the whole is much more than the sum of its parts' (see Mitchell 2006, 1196): the above picture is not simply a collection of tiles, but together these tiles form something new (a picture). Kwapień and Drożdż (2012, 118) write, "[T]he phenomena occurring at higher levels may not be a straightforward product of the lower-level structure and dynamics of the system's constituents."

To return to the example of the pistol: A pistol is however a *simple* system, not a *complex* system. The difference lies in adaptability: a pistol is unable to adapt to its environment, and unable to self-correct. When for instance a malfunction (double feed, stovepipe, failure to feed, etcetera) occurs, a human is required to correct the malfunction. Complex systems, on the other hand, are able to adapt, as Ottino (2005, 1842) writes,

> A Boeing 747-400 has, excluding fasteners, 3×10^6 parts. In complicated systems parts work in unison to accomplish a function; pieces are connected to each other according to a blueprint and the blueprint does not change. One key defect (in one of the many critical parts) brings the entire system to a halt. Not so in complex systems; the system may still function if pieces are removed.

The "quintessential paradigm for a complex system" (Maslov, Sneppen and Zaliznyak 2004, 530) is a living organism, which is able to adapt to its environment without outside control, for instance when the immune system creates antibodies to fight an infection. This happens spontaneously, for adaptation is encoded in the properties of the complex system. Amaral and Ottino (2004, 159) write, "The common characteristic of all complex systems is that they display organization without any external organizing principle being applied; a central characteristic is adaptability."

Although emergence is a key characteristic of simple systems, emergence takes on a special significance in complex systems. While in the case of the pistol, if we understand the parts and how they relate to each other, we can predict what the pistol will do: fire (or not). In simple systems, outcomes are predictable with a large amount of certainty. Understanding how some of the parts relate to each other make it possible to predict how they will interact, e.g. understanding how the trigger will release the hammer, which will strike the firing pin, makes it possible to predict that the pistol will fire.

The same principle does not apply to complex systems, where "Qualitatively, to understand the behavior of a complex system we must understand not only the behavior of the parts but how they act together to form the behavior of the whole" (Bar-Yam 1997, 1). Part of the problem with predictability in complex systems is that because they consist of "populations of adaptive agents whose interactions result in complex non-linear dynamics" (Brownlee 2007, 1), the *way* in which they will adapt is not easily predictable. With complex systems, predictability is replaced with probability: A does not necessarily lead to B, but can only be said to *probably* lead to B.[19] This emphasis on non-linear reactions is inherent in Kwapień and Drożdż's (2012, 118) definition of a complex system,

> [A] system built from a large number of nonlinearly interacting constituents, which exhibits collective behavior and, due to an exchange of energy or information with the environment, can easily modify its internal structure and patterns of activity.

Examples of complex systems include governments, families, the human body (from a physiological perspective), a person (from a psychosocial perspective), the brain, ecosystems, the weather, corporations, the Internet, communication networks, and financial markets (see Kwapień and Drożdż 2012, 118 and Bar-Yam 1997, 4). Civilization can be described as a complex system, and Herbert Spencer advanced the notion that societies could be understood as organisms (D. J. Watts 2011, 248) – in other words, *complex systems*. In all of these complex systems, emergence plays a defining role. As Watts (2004[2003], 25) writes, the brain is for instance,

> ... in one sense a trillion neurons connected together in a big electrochemical lump. But to all of us who have one, a brain is clearly much more, exhibiting properties like consciousness, memory, and personality, whose nature cannot be explained simply in terms of aggregations of neurons.

While simple systems can be studied by dissecting the system and analyzing its components, the complexity of emergence has a defining impact on how complex systems can be studied. Bar-Yam (1997, 11) writes, "[E]mergent properties cannot be studied by physically taking a system apart and looking at the parts (reductionism). They can, however, be studied by looking at each of the parts in the context of the system as a whole" (see also Luke and Stamatakis 2012, 358). This is a major problem with the current application of systems theory in the study of literature, but first we need to consider what a literary system is.

The literary system

Itamar Even-Zohar (1990, 85) defines a literary system as a,

> Network of relations which can be hypothesized for an aggregate of factors assumed to be involved with a socio-cultural activity, and consequently that activity itself observed via that network. Or, alternatively, the complex of activities, or any section thereof, for which systemic relations can be hypothesized.

In this definition, it is clear that the same interrelatedness is foregrounded, as is the case with Von Bertalanffy's abovementioned definition of systems in biology. The activities Even-Zohar refers to are those of role players in the system, which he calls the "institution," which denotes,

> ...at least part of the producers, 'critics' (in whatever form), publishing houses, periodicals, clubs, groups of writers, government bodies (like ministerial offices and academies), educational institutions (schools of whatever level, includ-

ing universities), the mass media in all its facets, and more (Even-Zohar 1990, 37, see also Verboord 2003, 262).

De Wet (1994, 19) writes that a view of literature as a system means that the focus falls on the entities and the dynamic relations within the system (as opposed to the individual characteristics of entities). Numerous proponents of polysystem theory have argued that it is during the interaction of the literary work with this environment that the literary text gains its status as 'literary,' i.e. 'legitimate' literature (as opposed to popular literature). Shavit (1991, 233) for instance believes, "A text gains a high status not because it is valuable, but because someone believes it to be valuable and more important, because someone has the political-cultural power to grant the text the status they believe it deserves." Jan Senekal (1987, 177-178) also argues, "a book that is not reviewed, and not reviewed by an acknowledged, vetted critic, can hardly be seen as literature, and be included in literary histories."[20] In his view, a (positive) review acts like postage stamp, "it mails the book to history, to immortality, and as believed earlier, monument-committees."[21] The views of reviewers who have acquired a reputation as experts of course carry more weight than the views of novices, and in some cases, these reviewers may even publish on reviewed works in academic journals, displaying their training and experience as *scholars*, further lending legitimacy to their reviews.

Furthermore, *where* the review is published also has an influence on the literary value of a text: Reviews published in respected journals are considered more prestigious than those published in small, regional newspapers, and indeed their ability to reach an academic audience allows these journals to bring literary works to the attention of *international* scholars. The readership of these academic reviews of course differ greatly from the readership of newspaper reviews: These are targeted reviews aimed at the very makers of the literary canon.

Apart from reviews, the publishing house that decides to publish a work also has a significant influence on whether or not that work will be considered literature in the future. Works published at publishing houses that have a high prestige value get more attention from reviewers, and are more likely to be considered for literary prizes. In Afrikaans literature, it has been shown that Tafelberg and Human & Rousseau are the most prestigious publishing houses (B. A. Senekal 2013e), as De Bezige Bij and Querido are in the Netherlands (Verboord, Janssen and Van Rees 2006, 295). Verboord, Janssen and Van Rees (2006, 290) write,

> In the longer term, the product of a publishing company, its fund, involves above and beyond economic value also symbolic value, which reflects on newcomers. The prestigious publishing house is called prestigious because it counts renowned authors in his fund. When the manuscript of a newcomer is published by such a leading publishing house, then that prestige reflects onto this newcomer.[22]

A work thus has made its way through a variety of gatekeepers before becoming a *literary* work. Upon submission, a publisher will review a manuscript before deciding whether or not to send it to reviewers. This decision will be based on a complex set of factors, including: Suitability to the publisher, quality (as judged by literary tastes), and market potential (which is inherently unpredictable, as the publishing history of *Harry Potter* shows). In addition, Jan Senekal (1987, 177) writes that manuscripts are judged in this phase as elite literature (literature proper), popular literature, etcetera, which will determine which reviewers the publisher will use. If the manuscript is deemed "good" enough and in line with the publisher's views – and possibly financially viable – it will be sent to reviewers. If these turn down the manuscript, the author has the option of resubmitting to less prestigious publishing houses, with an accompanying loss of literary prestige, but it may still be a success, or perhaps an even greater success than it would have been at the prestigious publishing house. If even these publishing houses turn down the manuscript, the option of self-publishing is always available, but very few self-published literary works become canonized literature.

If the manuscript has been accepted and published, it can be reviewed, or not. If it is reviewed, it can be reviewed by a novice, or a reviewer with a substantial amount of social capital.[23] If the former, the work may become a success, contributing to the prestige of the reviewer (who correctly judged the work), or it may not. If a reviewer with a lot of social capital reviews the book in a positive way, it can still be a dismal failure, or a success. If numerous reviewers see value in the work, and if it is subsequently studied, and prescribed to students, and if the author produces numerous works that are relatively equally highly regarded, it can be included in a literary history, thereby (at least for the time being) positioning the work in the canon. The canon is of course revised constantly, with some authors and works remaining, others written out of the canon, while new authors are constantly added (J. H. Senekal 1987, 170).[24] Senekal (1987, 81-82) writes, "The reviewer or critic, the literary scholar, the publisher or retailer, the teacher – they all determine what literature is and what is not. In other words, social actions decide and direct the literary system, not (just) 'literary value.'"[25]

Evidently, this process includes a complex set of possibilities, and at every point where a decision is made by someone, not only does a variety of factors influence that decision, but also the outcomes of that decision are not always predictable. If quality could have been judged by objective standards, or if even market potential could have been predicted with certainty, the first publisher that received the manuscript of *Harry Potter* would have published the series. Duncan Watts (2004[2003], 250) makes a different and much more elaborate argument, albeit to the same effect, remarking,

> Quality (which here can be interpreted as the adoption threshold), therefore, is an unreliable predictor of success, and even great success is not necessarily a signature of great quality. The difference between a hugely successful innovation and an abject failure can be generated entirely through the dynamics of interactions between players who might have had nothing to do with its introduction. This is not to say that quality doesn't matter – it does, as do personalities and presentation. But in a world where individuals make decisions based not only on their own judgments but also on the judgments of others, quality is not enough.

Similarly, when discussing hit films, Watts and Hasker (2006, 25) observe,

> ... the success of a particular entertainment product cannot be explained by any measure of intrinsic quality or even by 'appeal'—the fit between the product's attributes and consumers' preferences. Rather, when people are influenced by what others think or do or buy, their individual choices interact in complicated and inherently unpredictable ways.

Like scholars writing on the literary system, Watts makes the case that the cultural artifact acquires its popularity through the dynamics of the system, not through the artifact's intrinsic characteristics alone. Watts (2011, 231) writes, "[T]alent is talent, and success is success, and the latter does not always reflect the former."

From the above, it is clear that literary systems exhibit the same non-linear outcomes as other complex systems. Watts (2011, 142) writes, "[P]retty much everything in the social world [...] falls into the category of complex systems." Literary systems can therefore be expected to behave in similar ways to other complex systems, because "the dynamics of complex systems are founded on universal principles that may be used to describe disparate problems ranging from particle physics to the economics of societies" (Bar-Yam 1997, xi, see also Watts 2004[2003], 65). In addition, if literary systems share the dynamics of other complex systems, the tools used to analyze other complex systems can also be applied to literary systems, opening up the possibility of studying the literary system in a new way.

We return to the issue of complex emergence that characterizes complex systems. If the behavior of the system as a whole is determined by the complex relations between the system's component parts, it is insufficient to take the system apart and consider parts in isolation, or to consider only one relation (reductionism). Emergence in complex systems means that the behavior of the component parts change when interacting with other components; as Watts's example of the brain illustrates, it is of little help to study a brain cell when the researcher wants to come to a better understanding of consciousness. Emergence also influences how a literary system is studied: It is insufficient to study only texts in isolation *if* the behavior of the collective is to be understood better. This is not to suggest that the study of parts in isolation is inherently invalid: On the contrary, as the study of a cell is valid in itself, so the study of a single text is valid in itself, as long as the objective of the study is not to come to an understanding of the system as a whole. This approach to a literary text is therefore not problematic: Close readings of texts do not pretend to contribute to understanding the literary system as a whole. However, approaching texts within a systems theory approach is conceptually problematic: If *all* the relationships within a system are acknowledged to affect the behavior of the system (emergence), then it is insufficient to study only some relationships without considering the rest of the system. It is however impossible to consider all relationships within a system by relying on verbal descriptions, and hence, the impracticality of implementing the concepts of systems theory poses a conundrum: How to adhere to the precepts of systems theory *in practice*?

An example should be illuminating. In Van Coller and Odendaal (2005), the relationship between the Afrikaans and Dutch literary systems is discussed, using some examples of authors' engagements with both systems. However, if *all* the relationships within a system contribute to its total function, then using some examples are insufficient: *All* relationships need to be considered. This would however be highly unpractical: Considering every author that published in both systems, every editor that may have worked in both systems, every scholar etc. cannot be done – not even in a book, let alone in an article. Nevertheless, emergence dictates that the behavior of the whole cannot be deduced from observing the behavior of *some* component parts.

This is one area where network theory offers a considerable advantage over current systems theory applications in literary studies. Network theory allows the researcher to take into account literally millions of role players, meaning that every relationship within both literary systems and every connection within these two literary systems can (theoretically) be taken into account. However, although the method allows the realization of systems theory's precondition of taking into account all relationships, compiling sufficient data remains problematic: Finding *every* relationship is far too large for any researcher (or even a team of researchers) to do. Taking into account simply every book published in South Africa and the Netherlands (thus still ignoring linguistic systems and other cultural connections), is already a Herculean task. Hence, both traditional approaches and the network approach ultimately fail to address the basic injunction of systems theory by not taking into account all role players. Does this mean that studies using either polysystem theory or network theory are, then, inherently invalid? No. Some form of artificially drawn boundary is necessary in any scientific study. When Watts and Strogatz (1998) for instance studied the average path length in the film actor network, other social networks, companies, transport networks etc. all had an effect on their network, but these networks were omitted from their study because it is simply impractical to take into account every type of network and every role-player involved. The essential difference between network theory and polysystem theory is then that, quantitatively, network theory comes closer to being able to take into account all role players and all their relationships, although network theory does not take into account the details of these relationships (in a qualitative manner). On the other hand, polysystem theory is better suited to a qualitative description of these relationships. In the end, neither approach is perfect, but in the *complementary* application of both approaches, the strengths of both can be maximized, while they, to a certain degree, cancel out each other's deficiencies.

Is the literary system really self-organizing?

One important issue however remains unresolved: Up to now, the literary system has been described as a complex system, without suggesting a formal way of determining what a complex system is. One of the key characteristics of complex systems, apart from adaptability and complex emergence, is self-organization. This refers to,

> ... a process of continuous modification of a system's internal structure owing to which an order spontaneously emerges and complexity increases. This process is facilitated by interaction of the system with its environment. The phenomenon of self-organization is particularly striking in biological and social systems, where the cooperation and specialization of the elements occurs at different levels of

organization, but this phenomenon can also be observed in less spectacular ways in other systems and processes as well, like, e.g., in chemical reactions, in crystal growth, or in the formation of dunes. Due to self-organization, from an initial microscopic disorder a strong order emerges in a form of macroscopic structure and global activity patterns (Kwapień and Drożdż 2012, 120).

Albert-Lazló Barabási suggests a simple, straightforward way of testing for self-organization: The power law. The power law is dealt with in more detail in the next chapter, but suffice it to say that the power law predicts that many small events will be accompanied by a few large events, rather than the average (Poisson or Gaussian) distribution that is predicated upon randomness and predicts small deviations from an average. In Barabási's (2003[2002], 77) view, "power laws are not just another way of characterizing a system's behavior. They are the patent signatures of self-organization in complex systems." When the power law is found to exist in the literary system, it can therefore be proven that the system is self-organizing, which – along with emergence and adaptability – characterize the system as complex. This issue is discussed in depth in the next chapter.

Systems-of-systems

The above, however, only focuses on complexity on a horizontal level. Complexity also occurs because systems are embedded in larger supersystems, and consist of smaller subsystems, all of which interact on a horizontal level with each other, as well as in a vertical manner with sub- and supersystems. Bar-Yam (1997, xiii) refers to "an ensemble of systems," and Wilden (1980, 402) writes, "All open systems are necessarily related to other open systems and to their own subsystems, as well as to the differing levels of organization 'within' themselves as systems" (see also Viljoen 1986, 8, Heylighen 1989, 24, and Vilar and Ruby 2001, 11081). While living organisms can be described as "a quintessential paradigm for a complex system" (Maslov, Sneppen and Zaliznyak 2004, 530), the supersystems, to which living organisms belong, can also be described as complex systems. Levin (1998, 431) writes, "Ecosystems, and indeed the global biosphere, are prototypical examples of *complex adaptive systems*" (original emphasis). This concept of complex systems embedded within larger complex systems, or system-of-systems (SoS), is a near-universal characteristic of complex systems: Kwapień and Drożdż (2012, 123) write, "The majority of complex systems display multilevel structure organization, in which individual elements from higher structural levels are on their own complex systems at lower structural levels." The same structural features found between systems on a horizontal plane are also found on a vertical plane: Metabolic processes resemble citation networks, i.e. human social interaction shares a similar network structure with the networks that contribute to being a living organism, just as much as scientific collaboration networks resemble film actor networks (both social networks on a horizontal level).

The fact that the literary system is embedded in supersystems has long been acknowledged; Van Rees and Dorleijn (2006, 16-17) for instance write,

> The cultural field is embedded in society, understood as the set of interconnected dependent spheres: in addition to the cultural, particularly the political, economic, and social sphere. Embedding means that political decisions and social-economic factors affect what happens in the cultural field. Simultaneously, however, culture in itself also exerts an influence on society.[26]

Note however that systems may belong to numerous supersystems simultaneously (see e.g. Fokkema 1997, 180). Greyling (2005, 158) claims that financial factors influence the literary system directly, and Senekal (1987, 188-189) argues that the black publishing market during the nineteen eighties in South Africa discouraged writing critical, mature texts, as the market focused on the publication of texts for schools. Of course, *what* people read – as well as whether or not they read at all – is influenced by their level of education, income (buying books is not a necessity), and the state of the economy in general: Higher interest rates may for instance force readers to buy fewer books. In addition, the political climate may influence what authors write about, as well as how they are received: In Afrikaans fiction, most works that are considered literary dating from the 1960s onwards have been critical of apartheid, while many works of fiction from the late 1990s dealt with the Truth and Reconciliation Committee. The literary text is therefore embedded in the literary system, which is embedded in a larger cultural, political, linguistic, and economic system, and all these systems interact with the literary text.

In a similar way, the literary system is composed of various subsystems: Metaphors, character interactions, and relations between the words used to construct the text. Viljoen (1986, 12) for instance writes that the text is related to entities within, to other texts, and to their environment – a "drietal relasies" [threefold relationship]. Language itself – which can be described as one of the subsystems of a literary text – displays the same hierarchical structure, as Kwapień and Drożdż (2012, 130) write,

> Language has a hierarchical structure. At the most basic level, it consists of phonemes (spoken language) and characters or ideograms (written language). Typically, the number of either of these elements in a given language is small and usually reaches several tens (for example, in British English there are exactly 26 characters and about 45–50 phonemes in active use; the latter number varies depending on a source). The phonemes and characters group themselves in morphemes, which play an important role of fundamental carriers of meaning. The morphemes are not self-reliant, however. The function of the smallest self-reliant components of language is played by the words consisting of one or more connected morphemes. A higher level of language organization is formed by clauses and sentences which are the most important units of information transfer. In the case of written language, there can be distinguished also other levels of the organization hierarchy (paragraphs, chapters, texts, and so on).

It should therefore be remembered that although the 'classical' study of literature from a polysystem perspective focuses on the text's relation to its environment on a horizontal plane, it can also be studied as a system-of-systems, and its internal systems can be mapped with network analysis tools. For instance, character interactions can be studied using SNA, as well as connections between words or motifs. On this level, SNA has been applied to literary studies in more studies than is the case for literature as a system in terms of a work's interactions with the institution: Agarwal et al. (2012) examined Lewis Carrol's *Alice in Wonderland*, Moretti (2011) analyzed *Hamlet*, Rydberg-Cox (2011) analyzed character interactions in Greek tragedies, Sack (2006) studied Dickens's *Bleak House*, Newman and Girvan (2004) analyzed *Les Misérables*, and Alberich, Miro-Julia, and Rossello (2002) studied Marvel comics. Only one such study has been published in Afrikaans literature, where Senekal (2013b) discusses family relationships in Etienne van Heerden's farm novel, *Toorberg*. The current study does not focus on using SNA to study literature at this subsystemic level, but it is important to note that the application of network theory to the study of literary systems can be useful at the sub- and supersystem levels as well.

6.5 Entropy and intersystemic interactions

The complex system necessarily exists in an open relationship with its environment. Wilden (1980, xxxi) distinguishes between open and closed systems in the following manner,

> [A] closed system is one for which its context is effectively irrelevant or defined as such (e.g., the solar system, the cosmos as a whole); an open system, in contrast, is one that depends on its environment for its continuing existence and survival (e.g., an organism, a population, a society).

Almost every system in the real world, as opposed to the laboratory environment, is therefore an open system, interacting with its environment by receiving input and producing output. Jan Senekal (1987, 169) writes that the literary system is similarly open to influences from outside,

> Even Afrikaans literary activities do not exist in isolation

Theoretical background   37

but is intimately intertwined with the outside world and its thinking – to which it is indeed even electronically connected. This is now so much clearer than in previous decades, and already from the beginning of Afrikaans literature, there has been a very strong import from other literatures to Afrikaans, from both Western and African traditions.[27]

We return to the "quintessential paradigm" of complex systems: living organisms, of which Von Bertalanffy (1968, 39) writes,

> Every living organism is essentially an open system. It maintains itself in a continuous inflow and outflow, a building up and breaking down of components, never being, so long as it is alive, in the state of chemical and thermodynamic equilibrium but maintained in a so-called steady state which is distinct from the latter.

Von Bertalanffy's remark on steady states and equilibrium is important to understand the behavior and functioning of systems. A system's open relationship with its environment can be described in the terminology of non-equilibrium thermodynamics by referring to the concept of entropy, which is defined by the Oxford dictionary as "a thermodynamic quantity representing the unavailability of a system's thermal energy for conversion into mechanical work, often interpreted as the degree of disorder or randomness in the system." For instance: A fire will burn until combustible material (including oxygen) are exhausted, i.e. when no more energy is available to keep the fire burning.

The second principle of thermodynamics is one of the most important concepts in science, and according to Ilya Prigogine (1978, 777), it "has played a fundamental role in the history of science far beyond its original scope." Boltzmann's work on kinetic theory, Planck's discovery of quantum theory, and Einstein's theory of spontaneous emission, were all based on the second law of thermodynamics (Prigogine 1978, 777), and as the following section will show, it has bearing on our understanding of the literary system as well.

In a closed system, entropy always increases to a maximum according to the Clausius formula: $dS \geq 0$. This is based on the second law of thermodynamics, which states that, "in a closed system, a certain quantity, called entropy, must increase to a maximum, and eventually the process comes to stop as a state of equilibrium" (Von Bertalanffy 1968, 39). Equilibrium is characterized by "the minimum of the Helmholtz free energy" (Prigogine 1978, 777), i.e. because of the internal production of entropy, no free energy is left to conduct any work. The second law of thermodynamics therefore determines that the fire will die out (if in an enclosed space) – death being the final "state of equilibrium."

In an open system, entropy also increases to a maximum, but the import of negative entropy (negentropy) from the environment can counter the internal production of entropy to ensure a dynamic (as opposed to static) equilibrium, according to the Prigogine formula: $dS = d_e S + d_i S$ (Prigogine 1978, 778, see also 1997, 61). In this formula, $d_e S$ represents the change of entropy by import, while $d_i S$ refers to the internal production of entropy within the system. Prigogine (1978, 778) provides the following diagram of the interaction between system and environment in terms of entropy:

According to the second law of thermodynamics, $d_i S$ is always positive, but $d_e S$ can be positive or negative (negentropy). Von Bertalanffy (1968, 125) writes,

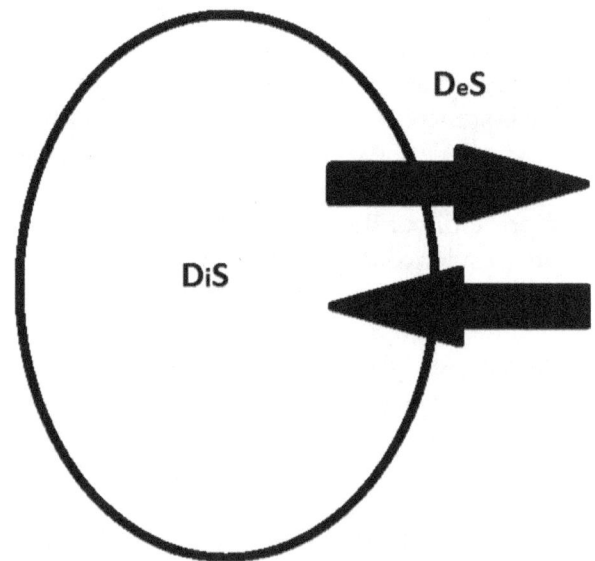

The exchange of entropy between the outside and the inside

A closed system *must*, according to the second principle, eventually attain a time-independent state of equilibrium, defined by a maximum entropy and minimum free energy [...] where the ratio between the phases remains constant. An open chemical system may attain [...] a time independent steady state, with the system remains constant as a whole and in its (macroscopic) phases, though there is a continuous flow of component materials (original emphasis).

According to Von Bertalanffy (1968, 191), "Biologically, life is not maintenance or restoration of equilibrium but is essentially maintenance of disequilibria, as the doctrine of the organism as open system reveals. Reaching equilibrium means death and consequent decay" (see also Viljoen 1986, 8). The complex adaptive system is thus dependent on feedback from its environment, which is, "the homeostatic maintenance of a characteristic state or the seeking of a goal, based upon circular causal chains and mechanisms monitoring back information on deviations from the state to be maintained or the goal to be reached" (Von Bertalanffy 1968, 46).

Feedback is a form of entropy by import: positive feedback reassures prevailing conditions and functions like d_iS, while negative feedback counters prevailing conditions and functions like negative d_eS. For instance: a fire will continue to burn as long as oxygen and combustible materials are available, producing heat, which in turn makes materials more easily combustible (as in the case of a forest fire). In this scenario, positive feedback can come in the form of a strong wind, dry grass, and a forest standing in the path of the raging fire. Positive feedback reinforces the current state, i.e. the existence of the fire. Negative feedback moves the system closer to a state of equilibrium, such as changing wind directions, natural obstacles (e.g. a river), or human intervention. Wilden (1980, 361) explains,

... for the open system the input received from the environment will be used to modify the output which the system communicates to it. The environment's reaction will be a function of this output and will consequently communicate a modified input to the system, and so on. Almost everywhere in nature and always in self-regulating mechanisms, feedback is negative. Negative feedback seeks to reduce the deviations within the ecosystem, that is, to reduce the difference between input and output. Negative feedback is therefore a control process tending toward constancy, stability, or steady state. But positive feedback is also found in nature, feedback which tends toward disequilibrium, disproportion, growth, change, and often destruction.

An example from a social system can perhaps be illuminating. The conflict environment of a counterinsurgency, likened to the spread of viruses by David Kilcullen (2009a, 35), is particularly prone to such a positive feedback cycle: Insurgents rebel against oppression, and the government clamps down on the rebellion, thereby providing yet more impetus for rebellion. Like the forest fire, the conflict state is maintained by positive feedback. Kilcullen (2009a, 115-185) then describes how negative feedback was introduced to the insurgency in Iraq in 2007. The insurgency had been in a positive feedback loop: insurgent attacks were met with US reprisals, resulting in civilian casualties, and thus sympathy was created for the insurgents' cause. Kilcullen however calls the majority of Iraqi insurgents 'accidental guerrillas', i.e. combatants who share neither Al Qaeda's ideology of a united Muslim state nor the war with the US, but rather fight for self-determination, service delivery and security, and thus the US could remove their antipathy if their concerns were addressed. During the Surge, US forces patrolled the streets in support of their Iraqi counterparts, thus avoiding the role of occupiers and the resulting miscommunication with the population. Furthermore, US forces policed their Iraqi counterparts, preventing Shi'as from abusing Sunni civilians, and vice versa, thus undermining insurgent propaganda that the Iraqi government was a Shi'a institution at war with the Sunnis. This helped remove the sectarian element of the fighting, and along with other measures and initiatives, including the local uprising against Al Qaeda, called the Awakening – which can also be deemed negative feedback – these reduced the level of violence in the country. Kilcullen argues that the positive feedback loop could not have been broken decisively were it not for The Awakening: although initiatives taken by US commanders did have a positive effect by introducing negative feedback into the system, the turning point came not from the US military, but from Iraqi citizens. The system itself thus introduced negative feedback – although guided by the US and Iraqi authorities, the population that drove the insurgency introduced their own negative feedback to undermine the existing state (the insurgency).

Feedback and entropy are important concepts in polysystem theory as well. In Even-Zohar's (1990, 17) view, a literary system consists of a hard core of canonized texts and literary models, which is "identical with the most prestigious canonized repertoire," as well as a periphery, which constantly threatens the core with innovating or marginalized literary models, authors and texts. Codde (2003, 105) writes,

> It is the dynamic tensions between the center and the periphery that guarantee the viability of the cultural system, because the center, which is usually prone to petrification and automatization, needs the renewal offered by elements penetrating from the periphery. If, for some reason, this renewal fails to materialize, then the repertoires used in the center become stereotypes and lose their vitality: the system is unable to evolve, and it collapses due to its inability to address the ever-changing needs of society.

This "petrification and automatization" can be compared with the production of entropy according to the second law of thermodynamics. Petrification and automatization *will* naturally occur in any cultural system, and if the system is to remain viable (maintain a steady state rather than a static equilibrium), the production of entropy needs to be countered with the import of negentropy. This occurs through a dynamic relation between the core and the periphery, where the latter is more prone to incorporate innovating models through contact with other systems. Even-Zohar (1990, 16) writes,

> As with a natural system, which needs, for instance, heat regulation, cultural systems also need a regulating balance in order not to collapse or disappear. This regulating bal-

ance is manifested in the stratificational oppositions. The canonized repertoires of any system would very likely stagnate after a certain time if not for competition from non-canonized challengers, which often threaten to replace them.

This conflict between core and periphery thus maintains a steady state or dynamic equilibrium in the literary system; a constant state of flux and conflict. Codde (2003, 106) writes that the periphery, "houses innovating models and repertoires that have not (or not yet) been able to penetrate the core of the cultural system as well as those that used to belong to the center but have now become obsolete." For instance, in Afrikaans literature, the model of the classic farm novel of the 1930s, characterized by a patriarchal system, ancestral heritage, the struggle between man and nature, etcetera, became petrified and automatized during the 1940s and 1950s. This petrification moved the genre from the center (as was the case with e.g. C.M. van den Heever's *Laat vrugte* and *Somer*) to the periphery, where it became popular literature, rather than literature proper (elite literature). Only when innovation was introduced into the system by writers of the Sixties, e.g. André P. Brink and Etienne Leroux, did the farm novel again enter the center of the literary system, albeit now in a different guise. The new farm novel challenged the patriarchal system, apartheid ideology, etc.[28] Entropy ($d_i S$) can therefore be likened to automatization, which is produced within the system itself. Art, as Shklovsky (2004, 16) reminds us, however seeks to make the familiar strange, "The technique of art is to make objects 'unfamiliar', to make forms difficult, to increase the difficulty and length of perception because the process of perception is an aesthetic end in itself and must be prolonged." Thus innovating models, genres, perspectives, and ideologies function as entropy by import ($d_e S$), which, in the literary system, is usually negative (negentropy). This allows the literary system to maintain a dynamic equilibrium: without negentropy, the system will attain a static equilibrium, which means death. Although it therefore may seem as if the system is constantly changing as new modes of representation and role players enter the center and are moved to the periphery, overall the system maintains a steady state: change is its constant.

Conclusion

This chapter has shown how systems theory sees the operations of a system, and it was shown how polysystem theory integrates with system theory applications in other disciplines. Central to the understanding of entities within a system is that their relations with other entities in the system need to be taken into account if the researcher wants to come to a valid understanding of how the individual text relates to its context. The more relationships that can be considered, the better, while keeping in mind that taking into account *all* relations is difficult in practice. This is where network theory is particularly valuable, for only through the network approach is it possible to take into account the large numbers of role players involved in the literary system. Quantity, however, does not necessarily trump quality, and hence there is still a place for more traditional polysystem approaches to the literary system, because when a researcher wants to drill down and examine individual relationships – while network theory is still valuable at this level – the qualitative approach taken by polysystem theory allows greater depth than network theory, while the latter allows greater breadth. The proposal is therefore not made here to supplant one approach with another, but rather to use both in a supplementary capacity. How network theory can be applied to the study of the literary system, is discussed in the rest of this book.

4

A macro level approach: The properties of complex networks

> I have always considered science to be a dialogue with nature. As in a real dialogue, the answers are often unexpected – and sometimes astonishing. (Prigogine 1997, 57)

In this chapter, the literary network is discussed primarily as a complex network, for although it is a social network that can be studied using SNA, it is also a complex network that has topological features in common with other complex networks. Through these universal characteristics, we can learn much about the literary network without drilling down to the individual node level. The next chapter uses a traditional SNA-approach in discussing the literary network at the node level, which Kwapień and Drożdż (2012, 210) call "Microscopic topological properties of a network," while the current chapter focuses on the macrolevel characteristics of networks.

Newman (2003, 174-180) distinguishes between four types of networks:

1. *Social networks*, e.g. a network of company directors, film actor networks, friendship networks, and networks of relationships in the work environment;
2. *Information networks*, e.g. the World Wide Web and citation networks in academic fields;
3. *Technological networks*, e.g. power grids, the Internet, company Intranet networks, and transport networks;

4. *Biological networks*, e.g. protein networks, ecosystems, metabolic interactions, and neural networks.

All these types of networks exhibit similar characteristics, and are in essence each a collection of entities (also called *nodes, actors,* or *vertices*) and the links between them (see Wang 2002, 885, Newman 2003, 168 and Dos Santos et al. 2012, 240). What these entities or nodes are of course depends on the network, which in turn can take a variety of forms, as Boccaletti et al. (2006, 177) write,

> Networks are all around us, and we are ourselves, as individuals, the units of a network of social relationships of different kinds and, as biological systems, the delicate result of a network of biochemical reactions. Networks can be tangible objects in the Euclidean space, such as electric power grids, the Internet, highways or subway systems, and neural networks. Or they can be entities defined in an abstract space, such as networks of acquaintances or collaborations between individuals.

Serrat (2010, 1) provides a more comprehensive definition of a social network,

> Social networks are nodes of individuals, groups, organizations, and related systems that tie in one or more types of interdependencies: these include shared values, visions, and ideas; social contacts; kinship; conflict; financial exchanges; trade; joint membership in organizations; and group participation in events, among numerous other aspects of human relationships.

Studies in physics usually distinguish between random networks and real-world, or complex, networks. The difference will be addressed in the following sections, but suffice it to say that real-world networks generally exhibit high clustering, the existence of high-degree nodes, the power law degree distribution, assortativity, and small-worldedness (see Guillaume and Latapy 2004, 215,

Amaral and Ottino 2004, 151, and Bullmore and Sporns 2009, 187). Note that these are *universal* characteristics, as Barabási (2009, 412) writes,

> ... probably the most surprising discovery of modern network theory is the universality of the network topology: Many real networks, from the cell to the Internet, independent of their age, function, and scope, converge to similar architectures. It is this universality that allowed researchers from different disciplines to embrace network theory as a common paradigm (see also Kwapień and Drożdż 2012, 120).

The universality of characteristics of real-world, complex networks implies that many of the same approaches can be used to study different types of networks. In the following sections, complex network theory is therefore integrated with SNA, for the literary network is clearly a *social* network (although also a *complex* network) that allows for both types of approaches.

Small-worldedness

Small-worldedness refers to the fact that although there may be millions or even billions of entities within a network, on average, a relatively small number of links need to be traversed in order to reach any other entity. This was famously proposed by Milgram (1967), who sent letters from subjects in Nebraska to a specific target person in Boston, and calculated the average number of links to the target as six. However, people are not able to distinguish the shortest path between themselves and the target – a detailed view of the entire network structure is needed to determine the shortest path. The data necessary to provide a detailed view of the entire network could not be gathered reliably before the Internet came, and in 1998, Duncan Watts and Steven Strogatz used the Internet Movie Database as a proxy for a social network to calculate an average path length between movie actors of 3.65. This means that every actor is only an average of 3.65 steps away from any other movie actor, as illustrated by the Kevin Bacon game, and indeed the Oracle of Kevin Bacon includes a Hall of Fame of people who found path lengths higher than 7, and none higher than 11.

However, the film actor network is a substitute for a social network (used for a lack of comprehensive data on social networks), rather than an actual social network. In 2008, two computer scientists at Microsoft Research computed the length of paths connecting pairs of individuals in Microsoft's 240-million-strong instant messenger network, and found that on average, people were separated by about seven steps (D. J. Watts 2011, 84). This study suggested that the same small-worldedness found in the substitute social network of film actors is also at play in real social networks, as Milgram had advocated. However, Watts and Strogatz were not only interested in social networks, as Milgram had been. Watts (2004[2003], 100) writes,

> Although we came to [small-worldedness] by thinking about friendships, and although we shall continue to interpret many features of real networks in terms of social ties, the phenomenon itself is not restricted to the complex world of social relations. It arises, in fact, in a huge variety of naturally evolved systems, from biology to economics (see also Strogatz 2004[2003], 256 and Bullmore and Sporns 2009, 196).

Small-worldedness is therefore a universal characteristic of complex networks, which includes – but is not limited to – social networks. Neurons in the neural network of *Caenorhabditis elegans* were for instance found to have degrees of separation of only 2.65, while the co-occurrence between words in the English language network shows an average path length of 2.67. Scientific co-authorship networks show an average path length of between 9.7 and 4.0, while food webs show an average path length of between 2.43 and 3. Albert and Barabási (2002, 50) produce the following table, which provides the average path lengths of various complex networks:

Network	Number of nodes	Average path
WWW	153127	3.1
Internet	3015–6209	3.7–3.76
Movie actors	225226	3.65
Ythan estuary food web	134	2.43
Silwood Park food web	154	3.4
Words, co-occurrence	460.902	2.67
Power grid	4941	18.7
C. Elegans	282	2.65

The average path lengths of various complex networks

A short average path length is therefore a universal characteristic of complex networks, and it is found in the Afrikaans poetry network as well. When the ties between people in the Afrikaans poetry network are considered, i.e. which reviewer or scholar published on which poet, the average path length between all entities in this network is 3.241, while the network consists of 321 entities with 812 relationships.[29]

Highly connected nodes

Viljoen (1984, 67) writes that the focus in literary systems often falls on determining which actors dominate the system. Degree centrality in SNA refers to the number of connections a node has to others; in other words, "the number of first neighbors of a vertex" (Donges, et al. 2009, 158). This is the simplest form of centrality in SNA, and takes only the node's immediate connections into account, whereas closeness centrality, Eigenvector centrality, and betweenness centrality take the entire network into account. Degree centrality is an indication of a node's activity in a network; the higher the degree centrality, the more that node engages with the rest of the network (Freeman 1979, 238). Degree centrality, in terms of a node-level analysis, is discussed below together with the other forms of centrality, for in this chapter, the focus falls on the literary network *as a complex network,* and hence degree centrality is used here in this context.

Firstly, in complex networks, some nodes of course have more connections (degrees) than others do. When represented in a graph, these nodes can be seen collecting activity around them. Consider for instance the network of protein interactions in budding yeast, which is discussed in Sun et al (2003):

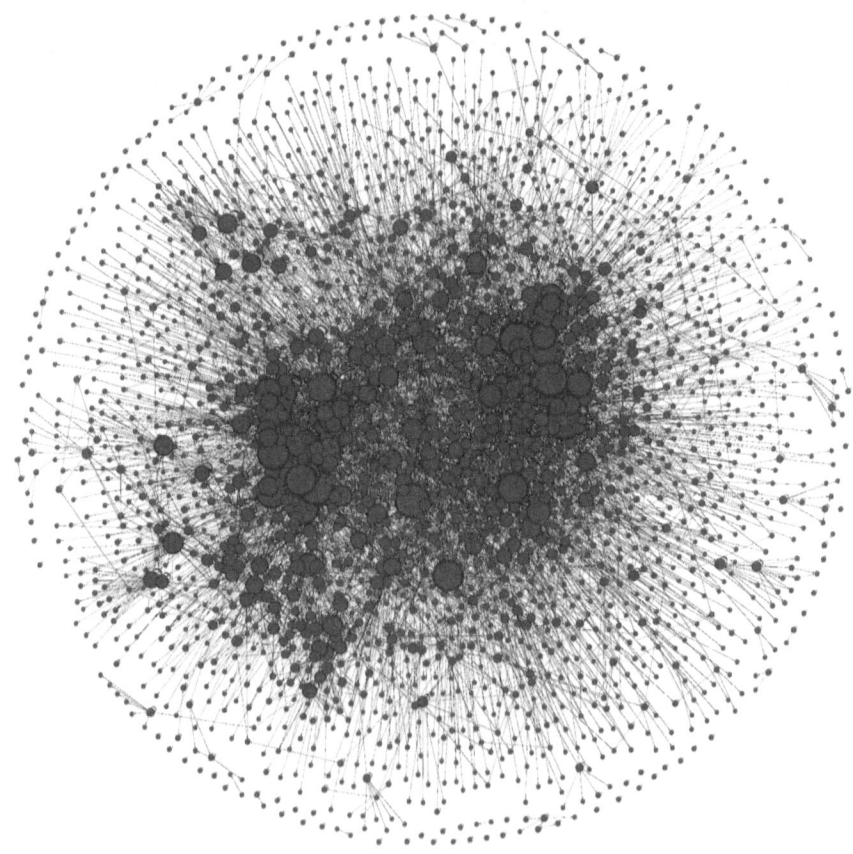

Protein interactions in budding yeast

Although this is a very densely connected network, some highly connected nodes can be seen (degree centrality is indicated with larger nodes). Even though the above is an example of a biological network, this topological feature is of course a *universal* feature of complex networks. The following graph shows the air transport network in the US in 1997, using data provided by the North American Transportation Atlas Data (NORTAD):

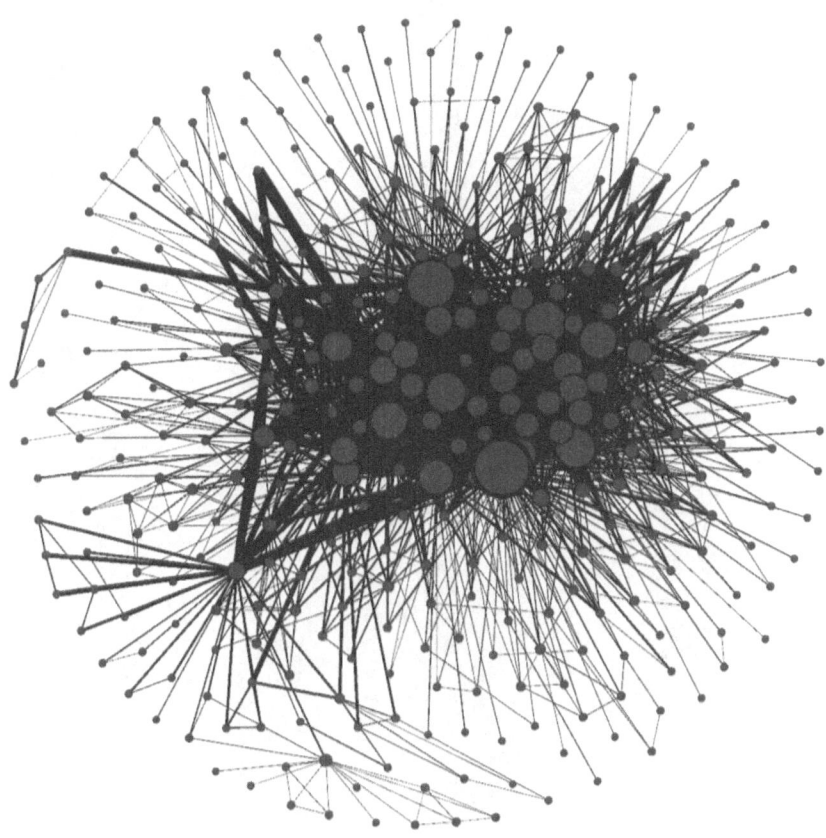

United States air transport network

52 Canons and Connections

Again, highly connected entities can be discerned when nodes are sized according to degree. The same topological feature can be seen in a graph constructed for the citation network within Afrikaans literary studies (2011-2012), as discussed in Senekal (2014):

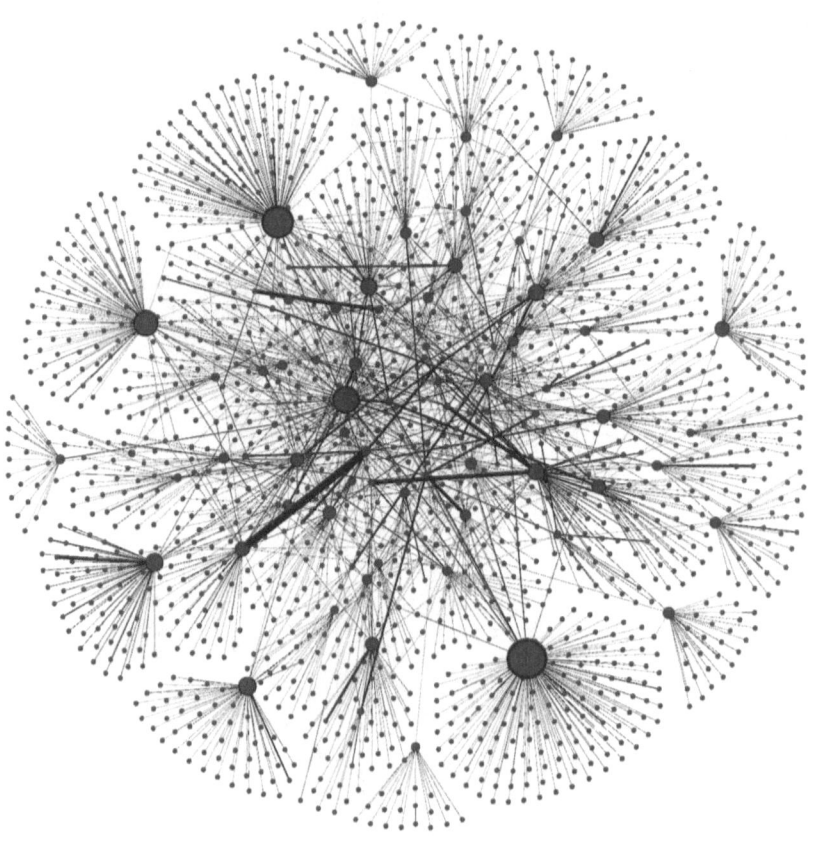

The citation network in Afrikaans literary studies

In all three the above cases, the presence of highly connected nodes can be discerned. Compare the above graphs with the graph of the Afrikaans poetry network:[30]

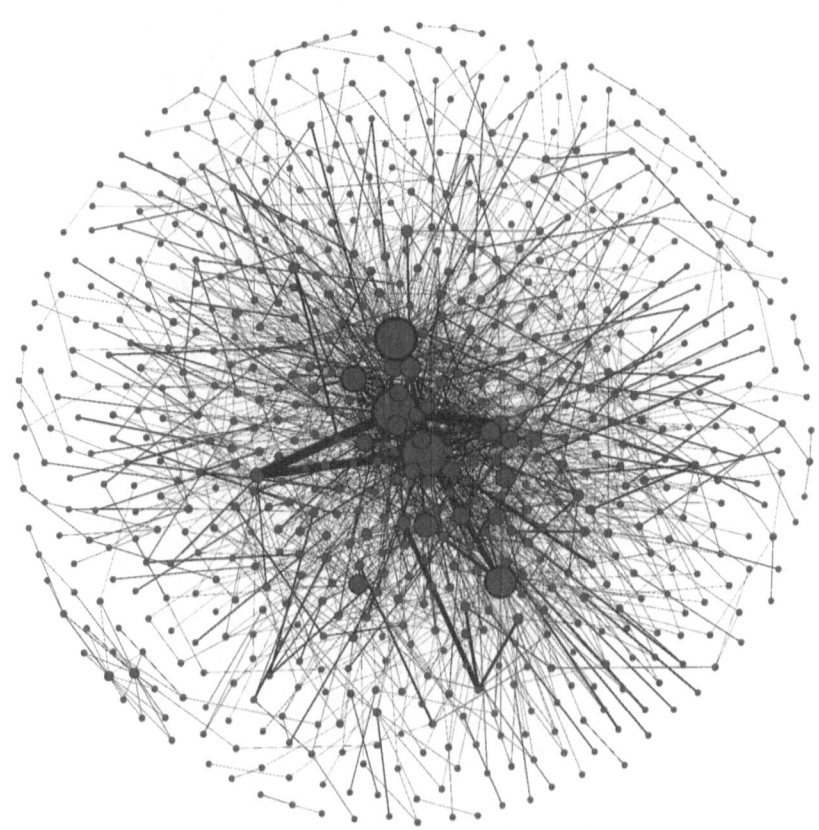

The Afrikaans poetry network 2000-2012

Of course, the center of this network is so dense that it can be described as a 'hairball,' i.e. an illegible network (Merico, Gfeller and Bader 2009, 922). Because this network distinguishes between critics and authors, poets, books of poetry, publication platforms where

54   *Canons and Connections*

reviews and studies are published, and publishers, the network can however be decluttered. In the following graph, only poets, works, and publishers are indicated:

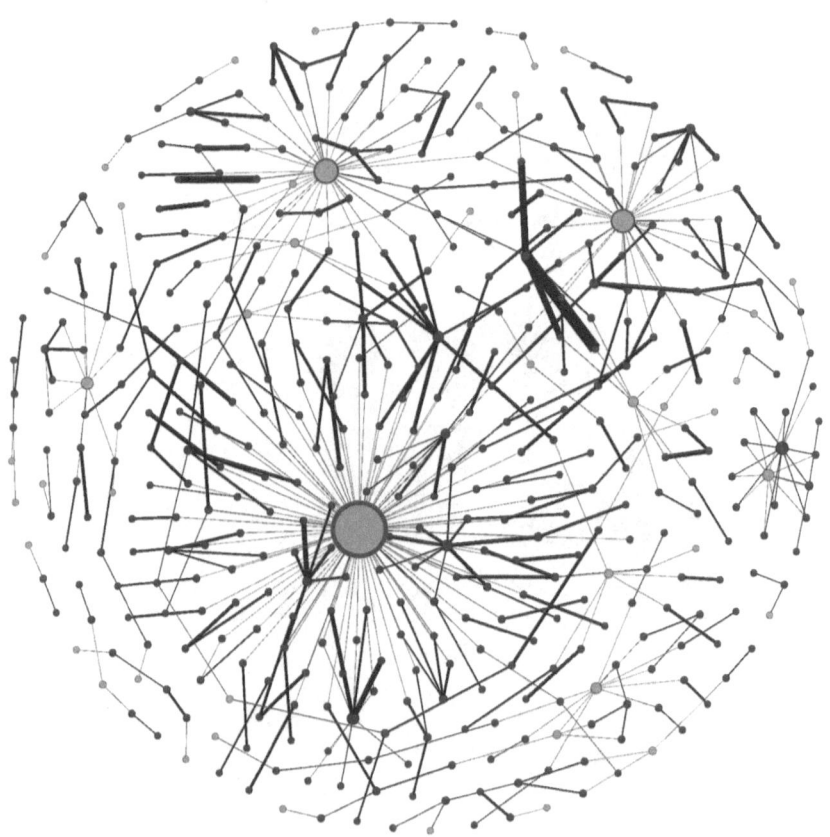

The Afrikaans poetry network 2000-2012 in terms of poets, works and publishers

In this graph, highly connected nodes are easier to identify. The largest node is formed around the publishing house Protea Boekhuis, which published the majority of poetry books since 2000.

A macro level approach   55

Another way to declutter the graph would be to consider only critics and publication platforms, i.e. where reviews, interviews, and studies were published:

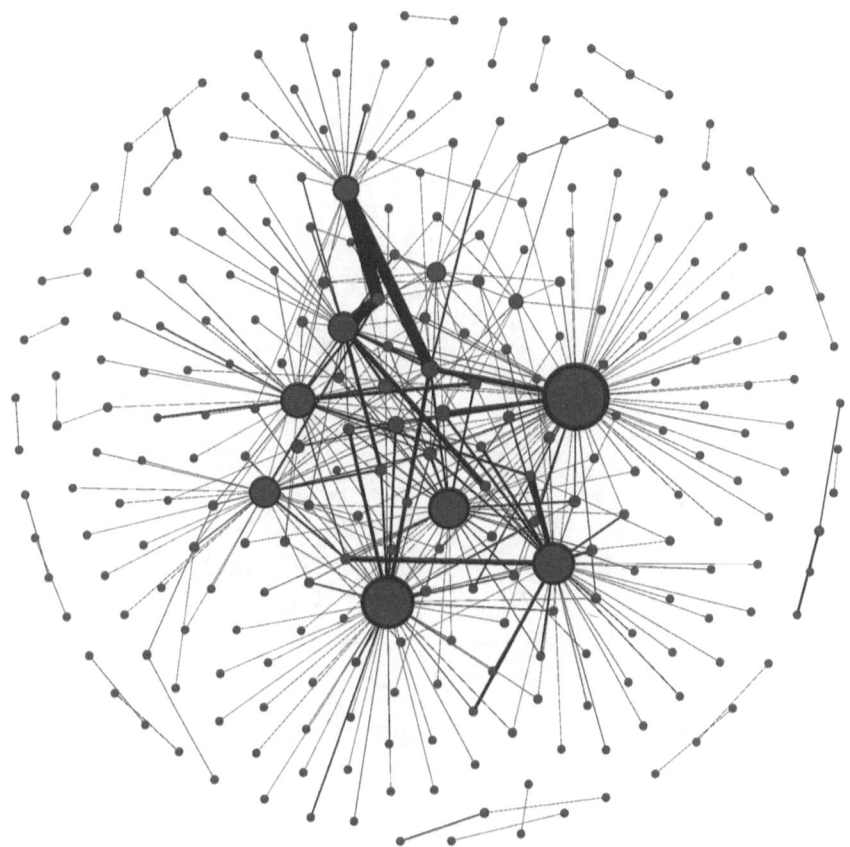

The Afrikaans poetry network 2000-2012 in terms of critics and publication platforms

Note that this network has many highly connected entities: these are the most active critics, as will be discussed in more detail in the next chapter, but their very presence suggests that a power law may be at work in this network (see next section).

56   Canons and Connections

Other experiments show that it is when works and critics are considered that the hairball develops, which suggests that critics often overlap on which works they review and study:

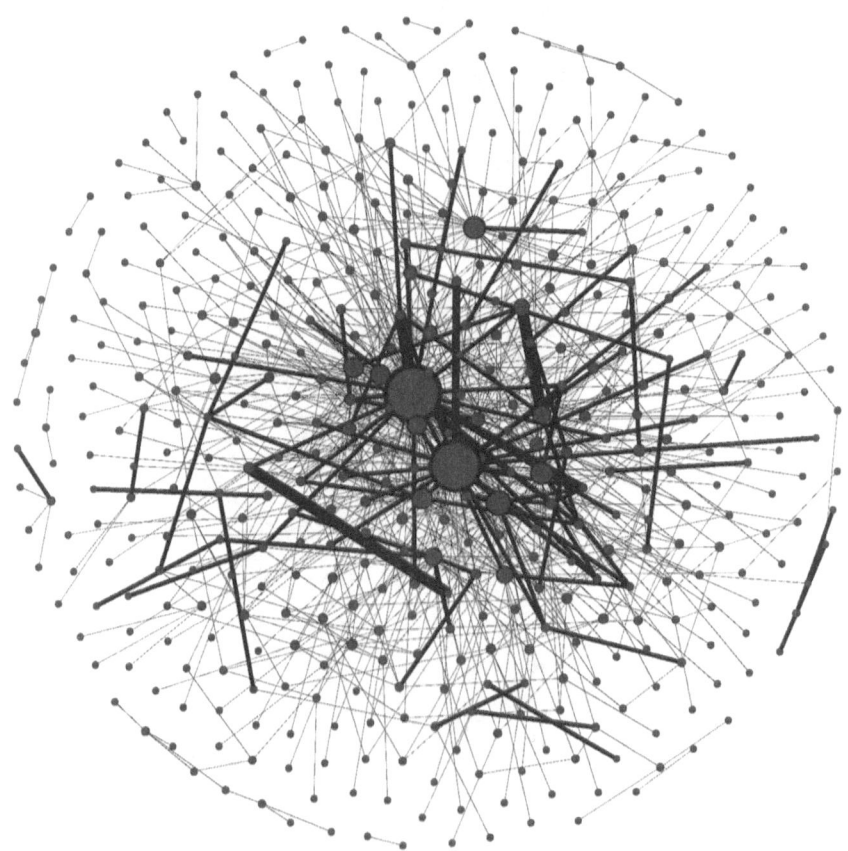

The Afrikaans poetry network 2000-2012 in terms of critics and works

In this instance, the hairball phenomenon indicates a very strong core, which will affect network robustness directly, as discussed below.

The power law

The Matthew Effect

Networks are classified as 'random' or 'complex' based on, amongst others, their patterns of degree distributions. Random networks follow the Poisson-distribution pattern (see Albert and Barabási 2002, 49, Amaral and Ottino 2004, 151), as modeled most famously by Erdös and Rényi (1960). In normal statistics, the majority of figures cluster around the average, according to the Gaussian function, to create the familiar bell curve.[31] Clauset, Shalizi, and Newman (2009, 661) explain,

> Many empirical quantities cluster around a typical value. The speeds of cars on a highway, the weights of apples in a store, air pressure, sea level, the temperature in New York at noon on a midsummer's day: all of these things vary somewhat, but their distributions place a negligible amount of probability far from the typical value, making the typical value representative of most observations.

Newman (2005, 323) mentions men's height distributions and average speeds of vehicles on a highway: in both instances, the vast majority of individual cases concentrate around the average. He provides the following histograms to illustrate (2005, 324):

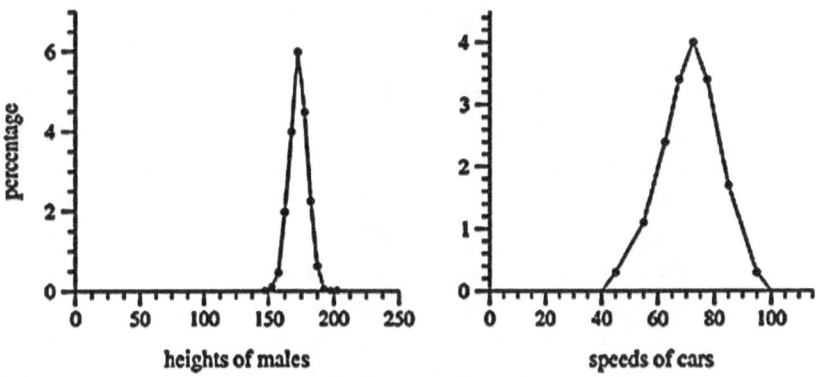

Newman's histograms of height and speed distributions

On the previous page, the figure on the left shows the heights in centimeters of adult men in the United States measured between 1959 and 1962, which peaked around 180 cm. On the right, the histogram shows the average speeds of cars on the highway, peaked around 75 mph. The histogram of population centers in the US, however, shows a different distribution:

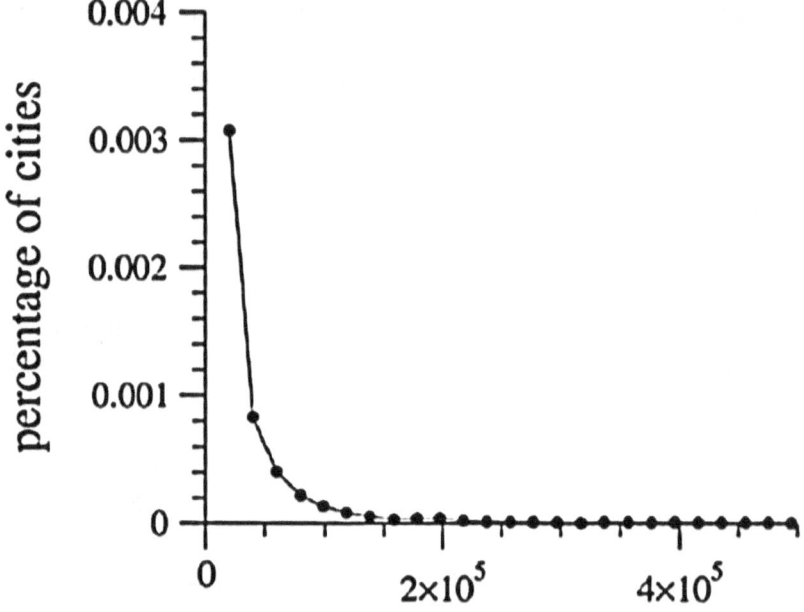

Histogram of population centers in the US

This histogram shows that a high percentage of population centers have small populations, while a small percentage of population centers have large populations. This histogram manifests the power law or Pareto's Law,[32] named after Pareto's (1897) discovery of the 80/20 rule, after having reported that about 80% of land is owned by about 20% of the population (O'Boyle and Aguinis 2012, 84). The distribution of wealth in a nation also usually follows Pareto's law, with the vast majority of wealth becoming concentrated in the hands of the few, while the largest percentage of the population accumulates little wealth. As Newman (2005, 325) however recognizes, the power-law occurs in a variety of systems,

In addition to city populations, the sizes of earthquakes, moon craters, solar flares, computer files and wars, the frequency of use of words in any human language, the frequency of occurrence of personal names in most cultures, the numbers of papers scientists write, the number of citations received by papers, the number of hits on web pages, the sales of books, music recordings and almost every other branded commodity, the numbers of species in biological taxa, people's annual incomes and a host of other variables all follow power-law distributions (see also Mitchell 2006, 1198).

In terms of networks, the power-law holds that most nodes will have few links, while only a select few will have a large number of links. The power-law is a law of probability, where the probability of a highly connected node receiving a high number of new connections is much higher than for a less well-connected entity. While random networks follow the normal Poisson or Gaussian distribution when the number of ties per entity is represented on a histogram, complex networks usually follow the power law.

One explanation for the power-law distribution is the Matthew Effect.[33] In 1968, Robert Merton suggested that scientific prestige accumulates according to what he called the Matthew Effect, named after the Biblical passage in Matthew 25:29, which states, "For unto every one that hath shall be given, and he shall have abundance: but from him that hath not shall be taken even that which he hath." Merton (1968, 59) writes, "The Matthew effect may serve to heighten the visibility of contributions to science by scientists of acknowledged standing and to reduce the visibility of contributions by authors who are less well known." The implication of the Matthew Effect is that those who have already accrued significant scientific prestige accumulate prestige more rapidly than those without, leading to an ever-widening disparity between 'major' and 'minor' scientists. Although Merton originally applied the Matthew Effect only to the accrual of prestige in academia, the effect has been observed in other fields as well. Watts (2004[2003], 110) for instance writes that cities grow in accordance with the Matthew Effect,

Large cities like New York, therefore, are more likely to attract new arrivals than small cities like Ithaca, thereby amplifying initial differences in size and generating a power-law distribution in which a few 'winners' account for a disproportionately large share of the overall population.

At the heart of the Matthew Effect's application to the study of complex networks lies an explanation of the Paretian degree distribution pattern, which is usually found in complex networks, and the Poisson or Gaussian degree distribution, which is usually found in random networks. The Matthew Effect shows that entities in the complex network that have many connections tend to accumulate connections faster than others, leaving an ever-widening gulf between the highly connected and the less well connected. Watts (2011, 72) writes, "[O]nce [...] a song or a book becomes more popular than another, it will tend to become more popular still." In Watts's view, books become popular because of a combination of intrinsic qualities, chance, the opinions of others, and a susceptible market. Once a book does become popular, however, its popularity alone can lead to it becoming even more popular, in the same way that Merton wrote that a scientist's reputation could be expanded in future because he is already respected, and in the same way that large cities attract new inhabitants faster than small cities.

In terms of node degrees in a network, the Matthew Effect can also be referred to as preferential attachment (Barabási 2012, 507), where a new node, rather than forming random attachments, preferentially attaches to an already highly connected node. Preferential attachment implies that "the more connected a network node is, the more links it will acquire in the future" (Barabási 2012, 507). This phenomenon first made its appearance in 1923 in the model of György Pólya, and guides network formation throughout diverse types of complex networks, "from Facebook and Google on the World Wide Web to protein p53, the 'cancer hub', in human cells" (Barabási 2012, 507). Barabási (2012, 507) explains,

> A new node joining a network, such as a new web page or a new protein, can in principle connect to any pre-existing node. However, preferential attachment dictates that its

choice will not be entirely random, but linearly biased by the degree of the pre-existing nodes – that is, the number of links that the nodes have with other nodes. This induces a rich-get-richer effect, allowing the more-connected nodes to gain more links at the expense of their less-connected counterparts. Hence, the large-degree nodes turn into hubs and the network becomes scale-free – the probability distribution of the degrees over the entire network follows a power law.

For instance, Buchanan (2003, 111) writes that preferential attachment or the Matthew Effect can also be observed in citation networks, "[W]hen scientists write a new paper, they are more likely to cite well-known papers in their field, those that already have been cited many times before, rather than obscure papers of which few have heard." In citation analysis, citations themselves form the connections between academic papers, and so 'the rich get richer' (in terms of connections). Mitchell (2006, 1199) writes, "Networks grow in such a way that nodes with higher degree receive more new links than nodes with lower degree."

The Matthew Effect shows how relations within the social system create success. Facebook did not have specific intrinsic features that put this social networking site above the rest, nor did the *Harry Potter*-series have a specific 'recipe' that made it a best seller (Watts 2011, 80), but rather these successes were the result of initial conditions that were subsequently amplified through the Matthew Effect. As Facebook became more popular, more people joined, because they could interact with more people on Facebook than on other social networking sites, such as Myspace. Regardless of personal preference, one tends to join the social networking site where most of one's friends are (in other words, the one with the highest number of connections to people), and for many people, that turned out to be Facebook. In a similar way, *Harry Potter*'s success meant that more people wanted to read the series, thereby its success in itself contributed to book sales.

In the literary system, the same rule can apply. We can hypothesize: When an author is considered canonized, his works are discussed in literary histories, and often prescribed to students. These students then undertake postgraduate research on the authors they know – often canonized authors – and perhaps publish articles from dissertations. Hence, these authors become even more visible in academic discourse. In the case of a new author, a first publication may not attract as much interest as a second publication, and if widely reviewed, a literary scholar may decide to publish a study on this author. Subsequently, the author's works may be prescribed to students, and then the proliferation of studies may follow along similar lines as a canonized author, leading to the author being included in literary histories. In other words: Often the choices scholars make on which authors to study has less to do with the 'quality' of the poetry, and more to do with what is popular (in academic circles) and what is best known.

However, the Matthew Effect does not deny quality altogether, as Watts (2004[2003], 250) writes, "[I]n a world where individuals make decisions based not only on their own judgments but also on the judgments of others, quality is not enough". The implication of Watts's argument for the literary network is that quality alone does not guarantee canonization, but also canonization is not a random occurrence: quality, together with fortuitous circumstances, and the dynamics of the system, lead to canonization. This view is in line with contemporary literary theory that views the literary text as a product of activities within the literary field or –system. The difference, however, is that polysystem theory makes no allowance for the Matthew Effect: complex network theory here informs *how* the literary network functions according to the well-defined principle of the Matthew Effect that results in a power law link distribution.

Works that have been studied in the past are more likely to be studied in the future, as the scientific field defines which topics are 'worthy' of study. For instance, this author has been reprimanded by a senior colleague for studying topics 'of which no one knows anything' – a reference to the author's publications on Afrikaans alternative music. The suggestion made by the senior colleague is that only 'legitimate' authors should be studied, in particular canonized and respected upcoming poets (not lyrics, which are not considered 'literature'). On another occasion, the same senior colleague remarked that another scholar's extensive publications on the poet Wopko Jensma are similarly inferior. This senior colleague focuses on poets such as N.P. Van Wyk Louw, Elisabeth Eybers, and Antjie Krog – all highly canonized and highly studied authors. What can be extrapolated from the views of this senior colleague is that some authors are considered more worthy of being studied, a phenomenon already noted by Jan Senekal (1987, 174). The question that the Matthew Effect answers is *why are these poets considered legitimate?* The Matthew Effect proposes that authors accrue prestige, but some – for various reasons including chance and quality – attain more prestige than others in the initial stage. Through a cumulative advantage, these authors then accrue prestige faster than others (as measured by the number of studies and reviews they attract), increasing their lead over the majority, and attracting new connections (e.g. new critics) faster than other poets do. This advantage over other poets is locked in after some time, and they become "the" poets – the 'legitimate' study-objects of Afrikaans literary studies. Watts (2004[2003], 109) writes, "The explanation of preferential attachment, however, makes an additional statement about the way the world works: that small differences in ability or even purely random fluctuations can get locked in and lead to very large inequalities over time."

Of course, authors will probably not be studied indefinitely, which is also predicted by the theory of complex networks: Albert and Barabási (2002, 81) recognize that nodes gradually lose their ability to attract more ties due to aging. In the case of an academic paper, except in a few instances of classic papers such as Erdös and Rényi (1960) or Granovetter (1973), a paper's citation rate diminishes significantly after around three years, and most papers will be consigned to oblivion in ten years or more. In terms of the literary system, authors may attract fewer studies as time goes by. An intriguing question is then what causes the degree centrality (because these mentions are links between authors and scholars) to age, and what prevents aging? One hypothesis again relates to citation analysis: as 'classic' papers continue to be cited despite their age, so 'classic' authors continue to be studied. The data considered for this study only record activities within the poetry network that go back to the year 2000, and hence a longitudinal study is not possible with this data set. Future studies could explore which authors eventually 'age,' i.e. who do not continue to be studied, and who do.

Lotka's Law

One of the most familiar concepts in science is that the vast majority of research outputs are produced by a small minority of researchers (Holliday, et al. 2013, 24). In a report on the state of research at the University of the Free State, South Africa, Johann Mouton for instance indicates that 21 authors are responsible for more than 50% of research output at the Faculty of the Humanities (Mouton 2013, 132). This phenomenon was formalized by Alfred Lotka (1926), who formulated his Law of Scientific Productivity after examining publications in the *Decennial Index to Chemical Abstracts* 1907-1916 and Auerbach's *Geschichtstafeln der Physik* submitted by chemists and physicists in the early 20th century (see MacRoberts and MacRoberts 1982, 443-444, Holliday et al. 2013, 24, and Chen and Leimkuhler 1986, 308). Lotka's Law states that the number of authors making n contributions is equal to about $1/n^L$ of those publishing 1 article, where L is approximately 2. Therefore, the percentage of all contributors contributing a single article is approximately 60%, the percentage contributing 2 articles is 15%, etcetera (Holliday et al. 2013, 24, see also Rowlands 2005, 7). In other words, a small minority produce the highest number of articles, while a large majority contribute very few.

Lotka's Law has been found in various other systems, apart from scientific fields, as Rowlands (2005, 7) notes, "The law has been found to be robust and pretty well universal in its applicability, extending beyond the world of scholarly publishing to even describe the productivity of software developers in open source systems."[34] It can therefore be hypothesized that Lotka's Law may be operational in the poetry network as well. Lotka's Law, in terms of the poetry network, could be described as the flipside of the Matthew Effect, and indeed Rowlands (2005, 9) opines that the Matthew Effect could be the mechanism that drives Lotka's Law. He (2005, 8-9) writes,

> This line of argument stresses that, independent of talent, authors require the right conditions to become productive: they need the confidence that feeds on success, access to research grants, freedom from teaching and administration, the esteem of their peers, access to specialist equipment, the

stimulation of teams of fellow researchers, and a supportive and well managed research culture [...]. These resources are all in scarce supply, and because publishing itself carries certain rewards (like credibility, standing), then there is a virtuous circle whereby these necessary resources flow disproportionately to those that publish more. But since competition for resources is so tough, only a few manage to break away from the rest of the pack.

In the poetry network, the Matthew Effect applies to poets, where literary prestige is accumulated at a much faster rate by some authors, while the majority receives little attention. Lotka's Law then refers to the productivity of scholars and critics, and suggests that some scholars and critics will be highly productive, while the majority will contribute a small number of reviews and studies each. The following table gives the number of scholars and critics who contributed *n* number of studies and reviews to the poetry network:

Degree	Number
1	125
2	37
3	12
4	7
5	12
6	4
7	6
8	2
11	1
13	2
14	2
15	1
18	1
20	2
22	3
26	2
28	1
29	1
65	1
68	1

The number of scholars and critics who contributed n number of studies and reviews to the poetry network

This means that one scholar or critic contributed 68 reviews and studies, while at the other end of the spectrum, 125 critics and scholars contributed only one review or study each.

In the form of a graph, it is clear that the degree distributions of critics and scholars follow a power law as shown above in terms of population centers in the US:

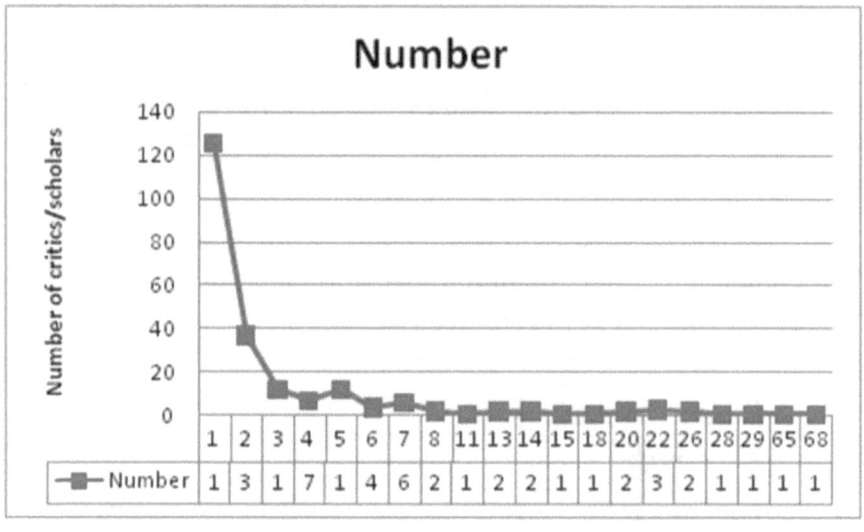

The distribution number of scholars and critics who contributed n number of studies and reviews to the poetry network

The above graph shows a clear fat tail distribution of degrees, indicating that Lotka's Law applies to the poetry network. Rowlands (2005, 9) writes,

> One implication of Lotka's law is that past publication increases the probability of further publication, for the reasons outlined above; it is very much more likely that someone who has already written 49 papers will write a 50th than it is for someone who has published four to write their fifth.

From the above, it can be extrapolated that there is a much higher probability that some critics will contribute more to the poetry network in a critical or scholarly capacity than one of the less active critics and scholars. The implication is that a few critics and scholars go to great lengths to contribute to keeping the network vibrant, while a much greater number contribute to a lesser extent. Who these critics and scholars are is dealt with in the section that examines the network at the node level.

An important point about the power law, which was alluded to earlier, is that it is the quantitative proof of self-organization, according to Barabási (2003 [2002], 77), "power laws are not just another way of characterizing a system's behavior. They are the patent signatures of self-organization in complex systems." This occurrence of the power law therefore offers the first proof that a literary system is in fact self-organizing. It was hitherto assumed that the literary system would be a self-organizing complex system, but the occurrence of the power law provides mathematical proof of self-organization.

Degree correlation

Degree correlation refers to the tendency of entities with a high degree to connect with other entities with a high degree – a form of assortative mixing (Newman 2003, 192-193). This is one of few topological features that differ in terms of the type of network under consideration. While social networks show a positive degree correlation (Conyon and Muldoon 2006), biological and technological networks show a negative degree correlation, in other words, "nodes with low degree are more likely connected with highly connected ones" (Boccaletti, et al. 2006, 182). It could therefore be expected that degree correlation should be found in the literary network, as it is – like the company director network – a social network.

The following table provides a list of the ten most highly connected critics and scholars, and poetry books:

Critic	Book
Odendaal, Bernard	Kleur kom nooit alleen nie
Hambidge, Joan	Verweerskrif
Crous, Marius	Groot Verseboek
Viljoen, Louise	As woorde begin droom, 'n keur
Cloete, T.T.	Die aandag van jou oë
Olivier, Fanie	Die algebra van nood
Beukes, Marthinus	die sterre sê 'tsau'
Bezuidenhout, Zandra	Oewerbestaan
Coetzee, Ampie	In die buitenste ruimte
Du Plooy, Heilna	Intieme afwesige

The ten most highly connected critics and scholars, and poetry books

How are these highly connected entities linked? As could be expected, there is a substantial amount of overlap between them in terms of the books they review. More significant, however, is in terms of *which* books they overlap; upon further analysis, six of these critics are found to overlap on the following books of poetry: *Oewerbestaan*, *Die algebra van nood*, and *Kleur kom nooit alleen nie*, and five overlap on *Wat die water onthou*, *As woorde begin droom*, *Ligloop*, *Die panorama in my truspieël*, *Van Roes en Amarant*, *Wanpraktyk*, and *Duskant die donker*. The ten most active critics (with the highest degree centralities), therefore review four of the poetry books that received the highest number of reviews (*Oewerbestaan*, *Kleur kom nooit alleen nie*, and *As woorde begin droom*). This shows that, to some extent, there is a degree correlation between critics and poetry books.

This offers an interesting insight into the workings of the literary network: Poets that acquired a significant amount of interest through the Matthew Effect, also receive attention from the most active critics, as suggested by Lotka's Law. The abovementioned senior colleague who reprimanded me for studying topics 'of which no one knows anything' does not feature in the above list of the most highly active scholars and critics, but his view provides an explanation for the observed degree correlation here: literary scholars and critics who want to be taken seriously should publish on poets that are taken seriously. And so the canon maintains itself: By determining 'legitimate' study objects, and those study objects defined by the Matthew Effect, the activities of the most active scholars and critics perpetuate the canon. Moreover, when new authors enter the system, when they are reviewed by these highly active critics, they move closer to a position in the canon. Degree correlation suggests that 'legitimate' critics and scholars study 'legitimate' poets, and their interaction is mutually beneficial: they reinforce each other's social capital. When overall network centrality is indicated with a force-directed layout algorithm, this mutually beneficial relationship between poets and critics will contribute to people's overall centrality, as discussed in the final chapter of this book.

Robustness

Robustness refers to a network's ability to survive the loss of some of its nodes (Boccaletti, et al. 2006, 213). In terms of robustness, there is a marked difference between random and complex networks: random networks are susceptible to major failures after losing nodes at random, while relatively robust against targeted attacks (the deliberate removal of specific nodes). The opposite is true for complex networks: while random failures have a very small influence on the network, a targeted attack on a hub or highly connected node causes significantly more damage than is the case in random networks. The reason for this difference is simple: the random removal of nodes from a network consisting of thousands or even billions of nodes is unlikely to remove any of the key nodes, as Albert, Jeong, and Barabási (2000, 380) explain,

> This robustness of scale-free networks is rooted in their extremely inhomogeneous connectivity distribution: because the power-law distribution implies that the majority of nodes have only a few links, nodes with small connectivity will be selected with much higher probability (see also Kwapień and Drożdż 2012, 207).

However, a targeted attack on a highly connected node will sever a much higher number of ties: "the error tolerance comes at the expense of attack survivability: the diameter of these networks increases rapidly and they break into many isolated fragments when the most connected nodes are targeted" (Albert, Jeong, and Barabási 2000, 381, see also Kitano 2002, 208 and Buchanan 2003, 131). As Andrew Haldane (2009, 11) phrases this issue, "a targeted attack on a hub risks bringing the heart of the system to a standstill." Watts (2004[2003], 191-2) writes,

> Ironically, the vulnerability of scale-free networks to attack is due to exactly the same property as their apparent robustness: in a scale-free network, the most connected nodes are so much more critical to overall network functionality than their counterparts in a uniform network. The overall message, therefore, is an ambiguous one: the robustness of a network is highly dependent on the specific nature of the failures, with random and targeted failures offering diametrically opposite conclusions.

This tendency of complex networks to be vulnerable to a targeted attack is exploited in SNA for military intelligence applications. The purpose in this case is to identify key players in a network, and remove them, thereby focusing resources on key individuals rather than the entire population – a continuation of the Phoenix Program in Vietnam, which eliminated the Vietcong leadership. On the other hand, the discovery of the vulnerability of scale-free networks has prompted government agencies to harden infrastructure against deliberate attack, e.g. hackers attacking the power grid or water supply.

Robustness can be illustrated with the example of photographs as used by Miller and Page (2007, 49), which is adapted here. Consider again the abovementioned picture, but with two additional alterations:

Robustness

All three pictures remain recognizably human, although they are very different. The core of each picture has however remained the same, and the alterations only changed the peripheral features of the picture. Actually, one needs to change a significant amount of features before the image becomes unrecognizable: an image can be said to be robust when random changes do not alter the image to the extent that it becomes unrecognizable.

In terms of the literary network under discussion here, betweenness centrality is one of the best indicators of a node's role as a key player (Borgatti 2006, 23), because it typifies that node as forming a bridge between nodes that would otherwise not have been linked. In terms of terrorist networks, Koschade (2007, 298) writes, "The node with the highest level of betweenness will almost certainly be the critical node within the network." In the poetry network, the critic and scholar Bernard Odendaal is indicated as the entity with the highest overall betweenness centrality, meaning that the loss of this entity would cause the most damage to the Afrikaans poetry network[35].

That is not to say that the network will suffer a cascading failure if he were to be removed from the network. Joan Hambidge is almost as well connected as Bernard Odendaal, and will surely take his place as the hub if he were to stop reviewing poetry, with Louise Viljoen and Marius Crous following closely behind in terms of betweenness centrality. The loss of a single hub does not often lead

72   *Canons and Connections*

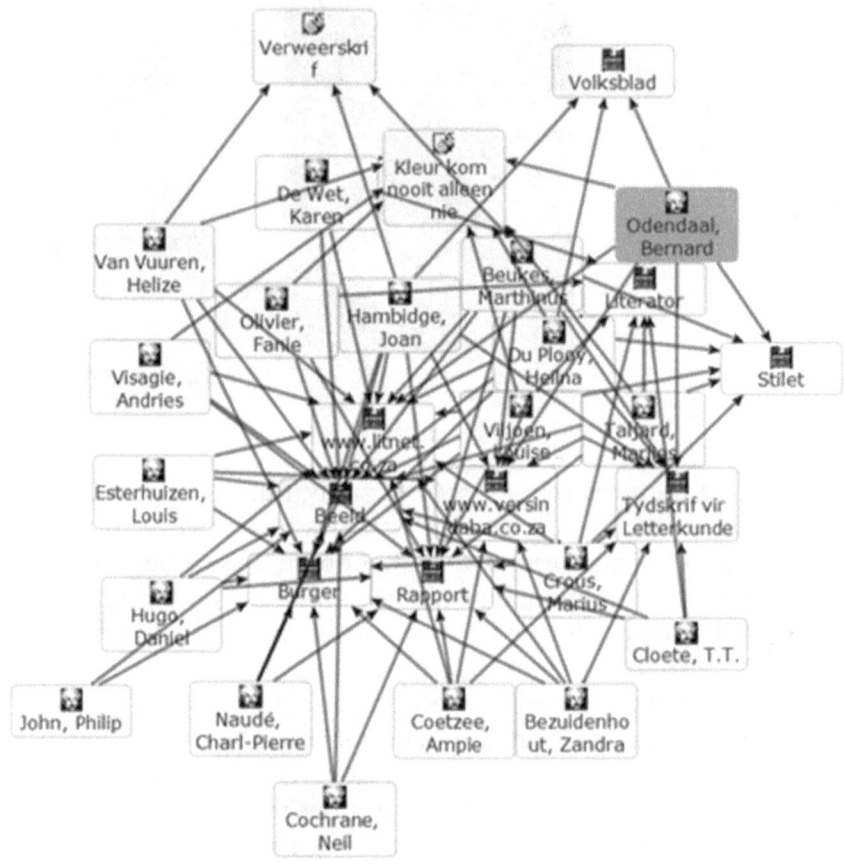

The hub of the Afrikaans poetry network

to a cascading failure, because ultimately, as Barabási (2003[2002], 221) writes, "No central node sits in the middle of the spider web, controlling and monitoring every link and node. There is no single node whose removal could break the web. A scale-free network is a web without a spider." However, if *all* the most highly connected entities were to be removed, it could cause significant damage to the network. Consider for example what the poetry network would look like if the ten most highly connected critics were removed, with the original network on the left:

A macro level approach 73

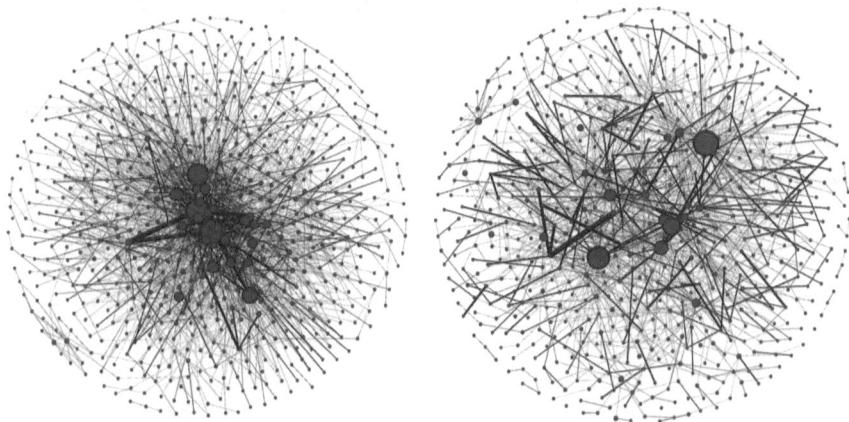

Robustness in the Afrikaans poetry network

Although the center of the network is now less dense, of course the network remains highly connected. However, if *all* the entities at the core of the network are removed, the network disintegrates into unconnected clusters:

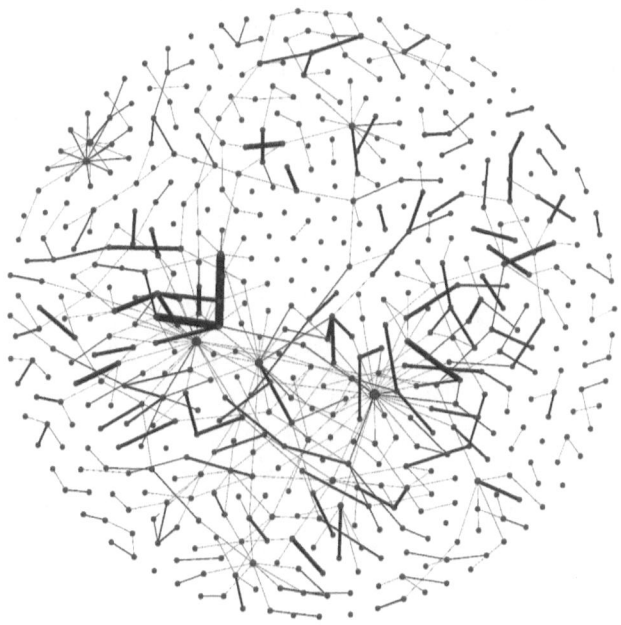

Robustness in the poetry network (core removed)

While critics are therefore important, the network does not disintegrate with the most active critics removed. Experiments with the removal of publication platforms and publishers delivered similar results to what can be seen in the above figure, and hence it is only when the entire core is removed that the network disintegrates. The poetry network can therefore be said to be highly robust.

Conclusion

This chapter explored the macro level characteristics of complex networks, and discussed these against the background of the poetry network. It was shown how the poetry network also adheres to the power law, and exhibits the same degree correlation, small-worldedness and clustering found in other complex networks. Most importantly, the Matthew Effect suggests a new way of looking at how literary prestige is accumulated, while robustness suggests that the literary system is not easily susceptible to destruction, even when a large number of key entities are removed. At this macro level, we can already apply the theory of complex networks in coming to a better understanding of how the literary system functions, but it is through a micro level approach that we can identify who the key entities in the system are. The following chapter therefore drills down to the node level in utilizing a traditional SNA approach.

5

A micro level approach: Measures of centrality in the network

Social network analysis posits that every individual is situated in a network of social relations, and that his position in this network is key to understanding how that individual functions. Emirbayer and Goodwin (1994, 1415) write that network analysis has what they call an *anticategorical imperative*, which refers to network analysis's refusal to see human action simply as the product of "class membership or class consciousness, political party affiliation, age, gender, social status, religious beliefs, ethnicity, sexual orientation, psychological predispositions, and so on." Rather than focus on the individual characteristics of entities, social network analysis focuses on entities' position in the network and the ties that sustain them.

In studying the role an individual occupies in such a network, Borgatti et al. (2009, 894) write, "At the node level of analysis, the most widely studied concept is centrality – a family of node-level properties relating to the structural importance or prominence of a node in the network." The most popular of this "family" of node-level properties include degree centrality, closeness centrality, and betweenness centrality – all centrality measures that were developed since the 1970s in SNA research, and currently embedded in computer software such as Sentinel Visualizer and Gephi. Everett and Borgatti (2005, 32) argue, "One of the main objectives of measuring centrality is the need to identify the most important actors within a network." This is one area in particular where SNA is helpful for military intelligence purposes: identifying key players in large data sets (Petraeus 2006, B-40). Following military intelligence and SNA's indicators of centrality, we can now start to drill down and look at the roles individual nodes play in the poetry network.

Degree centrality

Freeman (1979) proposed three centrality measures: degree centrality, closeness centrality, and betweenness centrality, all placing different emphasis on what happens in a network. Degree centrality is "centrality of activity" (Freeman 1979, 238); in other words, degree centrality identifies the most active nodes in a network by counting the number of direct ties these entities have with their immediate neighbors. When an entity has the highest degree centrality in the network, that entity has the *most connections* in the network, although this does not make that entity the best connected; "an entity may have a large number of relationships, the majority of which point to low-level entities" (FMS Advanced Systems Group 2013, 105). Petraeus (2006, B-43) writes, "Common wisdom in organizations is 'the more connections, the better.' This is not always so. What really matters is where those connections lead and how they connect the otherwise unconnected." The relative importance of an entity is based on his position in the *entire* network structure, and hence degree centrality by itself is not necessarily a measure of an entity's importance in a network.

The formula for calculating degree centrality for entity i is the following (Prell 2012, 97):

$$C_D(i) = \sum_{j=1}^{n} x_{ij} = \sum_{i=1}^{n} x_{ij}$$

Where,

x_{ij} = the value of the tie from entity i to entity j (the value being either 0 or 1), and thus it is the sum of all ties

n = the number of entities in the network

In the following sociogram, H has the highest degree centrality, as indicated with the darkest color:

A micro level approach 77

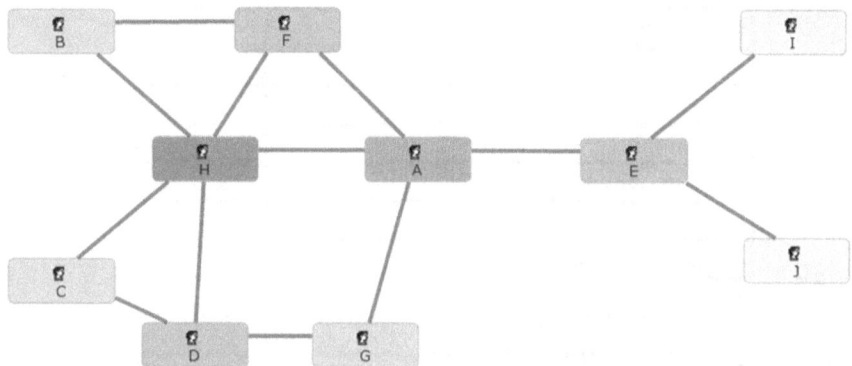

Degree centrality in a simple network

In this example network, H's highest degree centrality means that he is the most *active* in the network, but he is not necessarily the most powerful person because he is only connected directly within one degree to people in his clique, and has to go through A to get to the second clique (FMS Advanced Systems Group 2013, 106). Zhu, Watts, and Chen (2010, 152) however write that for organizations, degree centrality is an important concept,

> Organizations find it useful to know which of their members have high degree centrality, since these members are likely to be able to successfully diffuse information throughout their networks. It is often not desirable to transfer members with high degree centrality out of their networks, since this is likely to disrupt knowledge movement.

Because data on publication platforms, publishing houses, poets, and critics was collected for this analysis, it is possible to break down the degree centralities of entities according to category. However, because the network is so dense, centralities are better understood in table form than through a network visualization where degree centrality is indicated through colors. In the following table, the degree centralities of the publication platforms (websites, periodicals, and journals) with the highest degree centralities (2 and higher) can be seen:

Publication platform	Degree
1. www.litnet.co.za	67
2. Burger	51
3. Beeld	39
4. Rapport	38
5. Literator	31
6. Tydskrif vir Letterkunde	29
7. www.versindaba.co.za	26
8. Volksblad	22
9. Stilet	14
10. LitNet Akademies	9
11. www.slipnet.co.za	8
12. Current Writing	5
13. Boeke24	3
14. Meander Magazine	3
15. Boekeblok	2
16. Tydskrif vir Geesteswetenskappe	2
17. Zoutnet	2
18. www.roekeloos.co.za	2
19. Acta Classica	2
20. Mail & Guardian	2
21. Sarie	2

The degree centralities of the publication platforms (websites, periodicals, and journals) with the highest degree centralities (2 and higher)

This means that 67 reviews and interviews were published on www.litnet.co.za, 51 at *Die Burger*, etcetera. Therefore, these publication platforms are the most active in creating the contemporary Afrikaans poetry canon. Note however that www.versindaba.co.za only exists from 2009, and hence its 7th highest degree centrality indicates a much more active role than this table suggests.

The publishing houses with the highest degree centralities (2 and higher) can be seen in the following table:

Publishing house	Degree
1. Protea	93
2. Tafelberg	37
3. Human & Rousseau	33
4. Lapa	11
5. FAB	10
6. Selfpublication	9
7. Kwêla	8
8. Genugtig!	5
9. Suider Kollege	4
10. Bent	4
11. Quillerie	4
12. Suikerbos	3
13. University of Stellenbosch	3
14. Praag	2

The publishing houses with the highest degree centralities (2 and higher)

Protea therefore published the highest number of poetry books (93), Tafelberg the second highest (37), etcetera, which means that these publishers are the most active – quantitatively speaking – in creating the contemporary poetry canon. As the reviewer, who was alluded to in the preface, states, "A pigeon cooing 90 times in an oak lane will probably have a higher degree centrality than a lion roaring once in the same avenue. But who has the biggest impact / most influence?" Degree centrality alone does not measure influence, and confusing degree centrality with 'quality' or influence is a misinterpretation of the concept. Why then measure the degree centralities of publishing houses? Because it indicates an attempt to keep the genre vibrant, an issue that also has bearing on poets. The poets with the highest degree centralities (2 and higher) are:

Poet	Degree
1. Hugo, Daniel	9
2. Hambidge, Joan	9
3. Joubert, Marlise	7
4. Krog, Antjie	6
5. Breytenbach, Breyten	6
6. Vos, Cas	6
7. Esterhuizen, Louis	6
8. De Lange, Johann	6
9. Aucamp, Hennie	5
10. Marais, Johann Lodewyk	4
11. Walters, MM.	4
12. Gibson, Gilbert	4
13. Pretorius, Wessel	3
14. Gouws, Tom	3
15. Müller, Petra	3
16. Olivier, Fanie	3
17. Marais, Danie	3
18. Spies, Lina	3
19. Lombard, Kobus	3
20. Grobler, Mari	2
21. Laurie, Trienke	2
22. Van Rooyen, Piet	2
23. Myburg, Melt	2
24. Van Niekerk, Dolf	2
25. Bekker, Pirow	2
26. Bosman, Martjie	2

The poets with the highest degree centralities (2 and higher)

This means that Joan Hambidge and Daniel Hugo published the most poetry books (9 each), Marlise Joubert the second most (7), etcetera. Note however that no distinction was made here between original books of poetry, compilations, or translations, and of course, this is a quantitative measure, not qualitative: these are not the poets who contributed the "most," but rather the poets who contributed the highest number of works.

The critics with the highest degree centralities (10 and higher) are:

Critic	Degree
1. Odendaal, Bernard	103
2. Hambidge, Joan	98
3. Crous, Marius	44
4. Viljoen, Louise	38
5. Cloete, T.T.	35
6. Olivier, Fanie	34
7. Beukes, Marthinus	33
8. Bezuidenhout, Zandra	33
9. Coetzee, Ampie	31
10. Du Plooy, Heilna	30
11. Taljard, Marlies	28
12. Esterhuizen, Louis	25
13. Naudé, Charl-Pierre	22
14. Hugo, Daniel	19
15. Visagie, Andries	19
16. De Wet, Karen	16
17. John, Philip	16
18. Cochrane, Neil	14
19. Van Vuuren, Helize	13
20. Malan, Lucas	12
21. Pieterse, H.J.	11
22. Van Coller, H.P	11
23. Pakendorf, Gunther	10
24. Van Zyl, Wium	10
25. Vos, Cas	10
26. Grové, A.P.	10

The critics with the highest degree centralities (10 and higher)

This means that Bernard Odendaal contributed 103 reviews, studies and interviews to this network, Joan Hambidge contributed 98, etcetera. Again, quantitative contributions are not synonymous with qualitative contributions: these critics contributed the highest number of publications, not the "most" in terms of the promotion of poets, or to the understanding and value of poets. However, in this case some qualitative deduction can be made: publication platforms request reviews from certain critics, and it is unlikely that they would continue to request reviews from critics who do not write valuable reviews. While this qualitative element does exist where critics are concerned, the above table can however not be equated with a list of who produced the highest quality reviews and studies.

One of the most important questions is which books received the highest number of reviews and academic studies, because this points to which books received the most attention. The books with the highest degree centralities (10 and higher) are given in the following table:

Work	Degree
1. Kleur kom nooit alleen nie	20
2. Verweerskrif	13
3. Groot Verseboek	12
4. Oewerbestaan	11
5. Die algebra van nood	11
6. As woorde begin droom, 'n keur	11
7. Die aandag van jou oë	11
8. die sterre sê 'tsau'	11
9. In die buitenste ruimte	10
10. Oorblyfsel / Voice over	10
11. Intieme afwesige	10
12. Staan in die algemeen nader aan vensters	10

The books with the highest degree centralities (10 and higher)

The poets who wrote these books are of course also important: the sociogram on the following page shows the ties between poets and the ten books that were reviewed and studied the most.

The poet who received the most attention from critics is therefore Antjie Krog, who contributed three of the ten most highly reviewed books to this network. All other poets only contributed one book, meaning that Antjie Krog is currently the Afrikaans poet who attracts the most attention.

A micro level approach

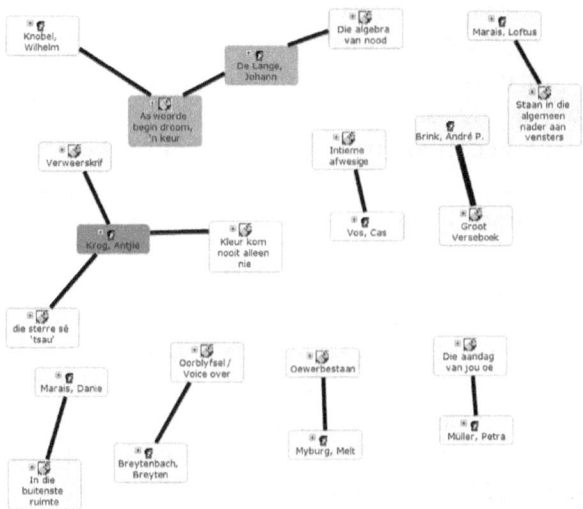

The authors of the ten books that were reviewed and studied the most

It is also important to note *who* reviews and studies Krog's works, as the following sociogram indicates:

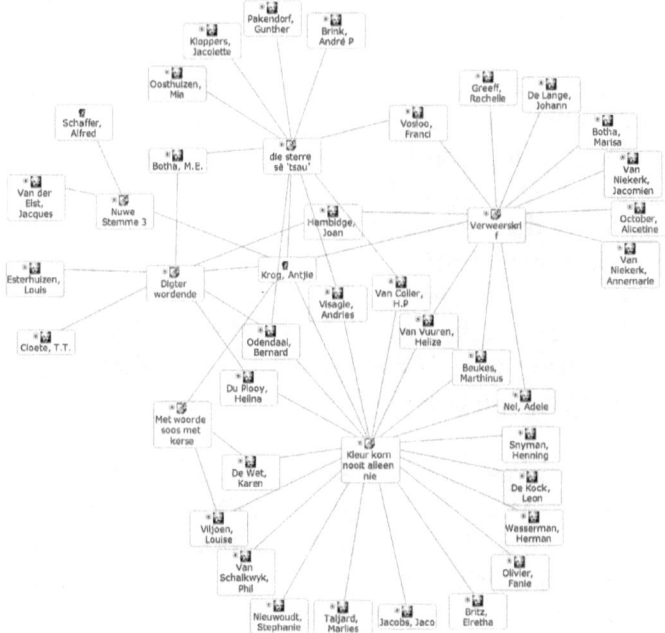

Krog's review context

Here it can be seen that Bernard Odendaal reviewed and studied three of Krog's works, while Heilna du Plooy, Joan Hambidge, Helize van Vuuren, H.P. van Coller, Marthinus Beukes, Louise Viljoen, and others published on two of her works. It is noteworthy that Krog's review context includes many of the critics and scholars that score highest on all measures of centrality, which suggests that she occupies a central position in the poetry network.

Betweenness centrality

While degree centrality only takes an entity's immediate context into account and offers a simple quantitative indication of an entity's activity in a network, betweenness centrality takes the entire network into account and has a qualitative implication, as Zhu, Watts, and Chen (2010, 152) write,

> Betweenness centrality goes beyond degree centrality to explain how powerful an actor is in a network. It is determined on the basis of how many other actors an actor is connected to, when these other actors are not connected to each other.

Freeman (1979, 221) defines betweenness centrality as indicating "a point that falls on the communication paths between other points [which] exhibits a potential for control of their communication." As such, betweenness centrality indicates positions that are "structurally central to the degree that they stand between others and can therefore facilitate, impede or bias the transmission of messages" (Freeman (1977, 36), see also Haythomthwaite (1996, 335) and Petraeus (2006, B-44). As Leydesdorff (2007, 1304) explains, it is this structural importance of connecting clusters that contributes to an entity having a high betweenness centrality,

> Betweenness is a measure of how often a node (vertex) is located on the shortest path (geodesic) between other nodes in the network. It thus measures the degree to which the node under study can function as a point of control in the communication. If a node with a high level of betweenness

were to be deleted from a network, the network would fall apart into otherwise coherent clusters (see also HafnerBurton, Kahler, and Montgomery 2009, 564).

Because of their privileged position that potentially allows control over the flow of information, betweenness centrality usually identifies the most 'important' nodes in a network (Boccaletti et al. 2006, 183 and Prell 2012, 107), and is related to Simmel (1922) and Merton's (1957) concept of *teritus gaudens*, which indicates that someone forming a liaison between people gains advantage from this position of brokerage. As Wellman (1983, 177) writes, "A gatekeeper, controlling access to an organization leader, often gains wealth, flattery, influence, use of organization resources, and personal pleasure in exercising control."

Betweenness centrality is calculated with the following formula (Prell 2012, 105):

$$C_B(k) = \sum \partial_{ikj} / \partial_{ij}, i \neq j \neq k$$

∂_{ikj} = the number of ties linking entities i and j that pass through entity k;

∂_{ij} = the number of ties linking entities i and j, and thus the betweenness calculation is for entity k.

In the following sociogram, A's high betweenness centrality is indicated with the darkest color:

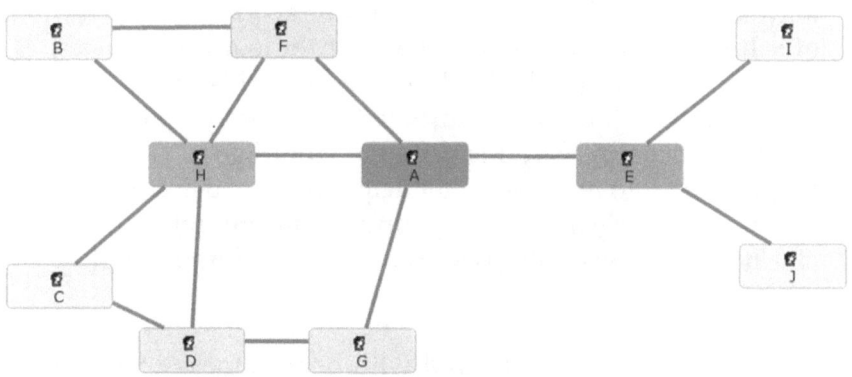

Betweenness centrality in a simple network

In this example, A has the highest betweenness centrality because he is situated between H and E, who are between other entities. H and E have a slightly lower betweenness because they are essentially only functioning as bridges within their own cliques, but they both fulfill important structural roles in bringing coherence to their respective cliques. Therefore, although H and E each have a higher degree centrality than the lightly colored entities, A has more importance in the network in other respects (FMS Advanced Systems Group 2013, 106). If E were removed from the network, I and J would be unconnected, and if H were removed, the cluster consisting of D, C, B, and F would lose coherence. In contrast, if A were removed, there would be two unconnected clusters, and hence, in the context of the entire network, A's connections are structurally more important than any other entity in keeping the network connected.

Granovetter (1983, 203) argued the importance of these 'weak ties' that link different cliques,

> The argument asserts that our acquaintances ('weak ties') are less likely to be socially involved with one another than are our close friends ('strong ties').... The overall social structural picture suggested by this argument can be seen by considering the situation of some arbitrarily selected individual – call him or her 'Ego'" Ego will have a collection of close-knit friends, most of whom are in touch with one another – a densely knit 'clump' of social structure. In addition, Ego will have a collection of acquaintances, few of whom know one another. Each of these acquaintances, however, is likely to have close friends in his or her own right and therefore to be enmeshed in a closely knit clump of social structure, but one different from Ego's. The weak tie between Ego and his or her acquaintance, therefore, becomes not merely a trivial acquaintance tie, but rather a crucial bridge between the two densely knit clumps of close friends.

Weak ties are thus also measured with betweenness centrality, as they provide structural connections between different clusters. The following table gives the betweenness centralities of publication platforms (those entities not on the list have betweenness centrality scores of 0):

Publication platform	Betweenness
1. www.litnet.co.za	0.643
2. Burger	0.4739
3. Beeld	0.2928
4. Literator	0.2079
5. Tydskrif vir Letterkunde	0.2013
6. Rapport	0.1679
7. Volksblad	0.1348
8. www.versindaba.co.za	0.134
9. Stilet	0.0386
10. www.slipnet.co.za	0.0197
11. LitNet Akademies	0.0186
12. Zoutnet	0.0135
13. Current Writing	0.005
14. Boeke24	0.0007
15. Meander Magazine	0.0006
16. www.roekeloos.co.za	0.0005
17. Acta Classica	0.0005
18. Tydskrif vir Geesteswetenskappe	0.0004
19. Boekeblok	0.0002
20. Mail & Guardian	0.0001
21. Sarie	0.0001

The betweenness centralities of publication platforms

This means that these publication platforms play the biggest role in providing structural coherence to the poetry network, and they contribute the most new information to the network.

The following table gives the betweenness centralities of the ten publishing houses with the highest betweenness centralities.

This means that these are the publishers that provide the largest measure of structural coherence in this network by bringing po-

Publishing house	Betweenness
1. Protea	0.6043
2. Human & Rousseau	0.1735
3. Tafelberg	0.1702
4. Self publication	0.1018
5. FAB	0.0415
6. Lapa	0.0279
7. Genugtig!	0.0147
8. Bent	0.0127
9. Kwêla	0.0061
10. Suikerbos	0.0018
11. Praag	0.0011
12. Quillerie	0.0008
13. Suider Kollege	0.0007
14. University of Stellenbosch	0.0004

The betweenness centralities of the ten publishing houses with the highest betweenness centralities

ets into contact with the rest of the network. This implies nothing about the artistic merit of individual books: Betweenness centrality in this instance signifies bringing in fresh, new material that keeps the system vibrant. It is no coincidence that self-publications score the fourth highest on betweenness centrality: Self-publications constitute a publication outlet that would otherwise not have been there, displaying the works of poets that would otherwise have been omitted from the network. FAB Publishers is another publishing house that illustrates what betweenness centrality calculates. Their position is indicated with the X in the following sociogram.

FAB is therefore positioned far from the core of this network, but play an important role in publishing the works of Floris A. Brown, which would otherwise not have been part of the poetry network. While Brown is himself peripheral to the poetry network (he is positioned just to the left of FAB), his works nevertheless contribute to the network, and this contribution is facilitated by FAB.

A micro level approach 89

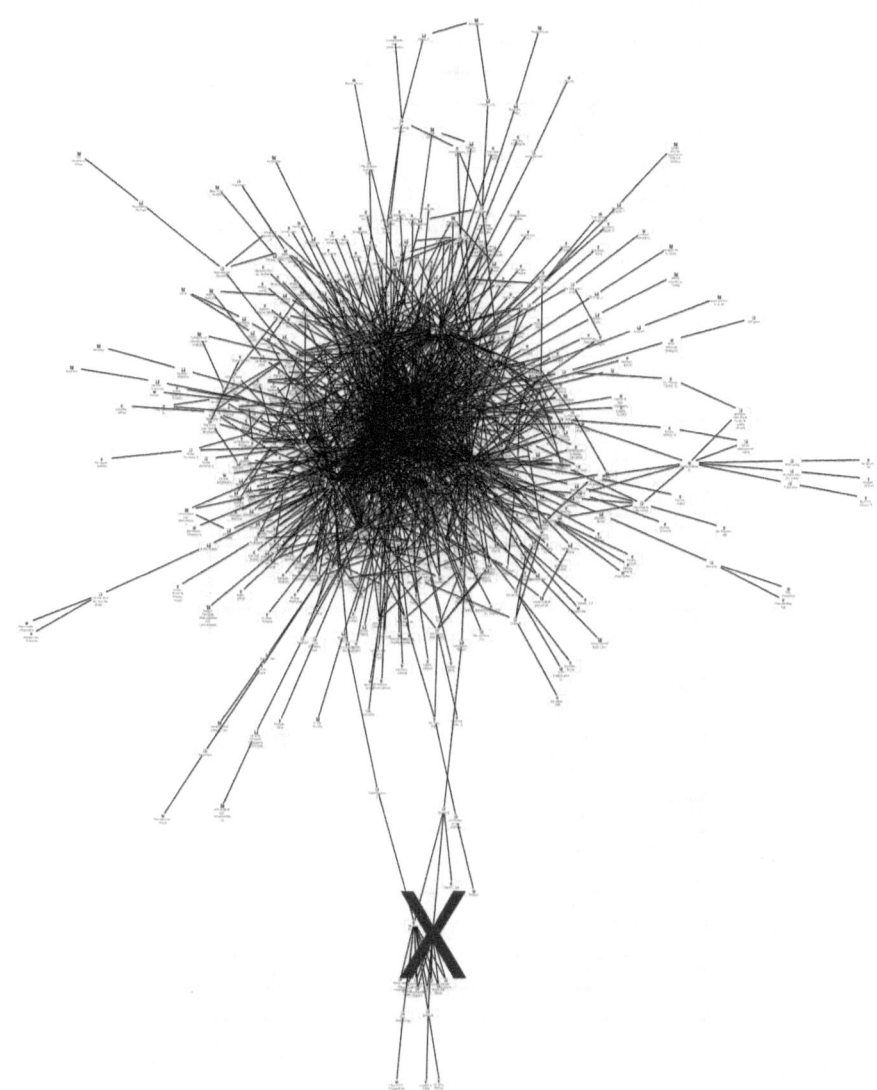

The position of FAB Publishers in the network

The following table gives the betweenness centralities of the 30 highest-scoring critics and scholars:

Critic	Betweenness
1. Odendaal, Bernard	1
2. Hambidge, Joan	0.9438
3. Crous, Marius	0.2458
4. Viljoen, Louise	0.2027
5. Du Plooy, Heilna	0.1825
6. Olivier, Fanie	0.1742
7. Esterhuizen, Louis	0.1649
8. Cloete, T.T.	0.1478
9. Bezuidenhout, Zandra	0.1475
10. Beukes, Marthinus	0.1283
11. Coetzee, Ampie	0.1228
12. Taljard, Marlies	0.1191
13. Le Cordeur, Michael	0.099
14. John, Philip	0.0722
15. Naudé, Charl-Pierre	0.0677
16. Hugo, Daniel	0.0484
17. Visagie, Andries	0.0476
18. Marais, Johann Lodewyk	0.0434
19. Van Wyk, Steward	0.0407
20. Malan, Lucas	0.0384
21. Van Vuuren, Helize	0.0383
22. De Wet, Karen	0.0342
23. Van der Elst, Jacques	0.0261
24. Pakendorf, Gunther	0.0254
25. De Lange, Johann	0.0227
26. Van Niekerk, Jacomien	0.0227
27. Slippers, Bibi	0.0226
28. Pieterse, H.J.	0.0223
29. Cochrane, Neil	0.0221
30. Smith, Susan	0.0207

The betweenness centralities of the 30 highest-scoring critics and scholars

Note the betweenness centrality score of 1 in the case of Bernard Odendaal: this signifies that he has the highest betweenness centrality of all entities in this network, including poets, publishers, publication platforms, books, and critics (1 is the highest betweenness centrality that can be achieved when centralities are normalized).

He is thus structurally in the best position to bring coherence to the network, which means that he plays the greatest role in bringing together poets and publication platforms that would otherwise not have been as connected within the network.

The following table gives the betweenness centralities of the nineteen poets with the highest betweenness centralities:

Poet	Betweenness
1. Hugo, Daniel	0.0082
2. Hambidge Joan	0.0063
3. Krog, Antjie	0.0057
4. Pretorius, Wessel	0.0052
5. Marais, Johann Lodewyk	0.0048
6. Gouws, Tom	0.0029
7. Breytenbach, Breyten	0.0024
8. Müller, Petra	0.0018
9. Vos, Cas	0.0015
10. Joubert, Marlise	0.0014
11. Esterhuizen, Louis	0.0013
12. De Lange, Johann	0.0009
13. Olivier, Fanie	0.0009
14. Aucamp, Hennie	0.0007
15. Walters, MM.	0.0004
16. Grobler, Mari	0.0002
17. Gibson, Gilbert	0.0002
18. Marais, Danie	0.0002
19. Spies, Lina	0.0001

The betweenness centralities of the nineteen poets with the highest betweenness centralities

This table means that these are the poets who bring together the highest number of critics and publishers, which could mean fresh perspectives on poetry, as well as further-reach for Afrikaans poetry in terms of where studies and reviews of Afrikaans poetry are published.

Closeness centrality

Closeness centrality is another of the three 'classic' centrality measures developed by Freeman, and "captures the extent to which the focal vertex has short paths to all other vertices within the graph" (Butts 2008, 23). Closeness centrality indicates a node's independence in a network (Prell 2012, 107), and "measures how quickly an entity can access more entities in a network" (FMS Advanced Systems Group 2013, 106). Closeness centrality is calculated with the following formula (Prell 2012, 108):

$C_c(i) = \sum d_{ij}$ where d_{ij} = the distance connecting entity i to entity j.

In the following sociogram, A has the highest closeness centrality, as again indicated with the darkest color:

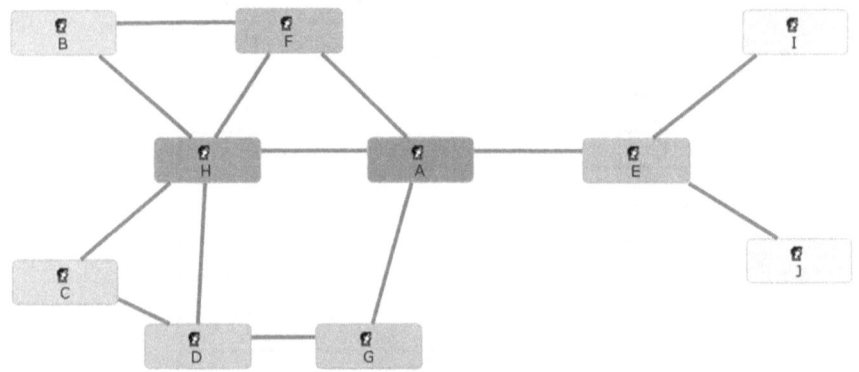

Closeness centrality in a simple network

A has the highest closeness centrality because he can reach more entities through shorter paths. As such, A's placement allows him to connect to entities in his own clique, and to entities that span cliques (FMS Advanced Systems Group 2013, 107), which also means that A is the least dependent on any one entity for maintaining contact with the highest number of other entities.

Closeness centrality also indicates overall network centrality, because entities found at the center of the network have, on average, shorter paths to all other entities in a network than those on the periphery. Take for instance someone who lives near Oxford Circus in London: On average, traveling to Heathrow, Stratford, Wimbledon, Canary Wharf, and Camden will involve a shorter journey than for someone who lives in Kew Gardens. The same principle applies in networks: reaching every other entity, on average, with a short path – which is precisely what closeness centrality measures – necessarily means a position at the center of the network. Overall centrality will be discussed in more detail in the next chapter.

The following table gives the closeness centralities of the 30 poetry books with the highest closeness centralities, from high to low:

Work	Closeness
1. Oewerbestaan	0.8813
2. Toevallige tekens	0.8754
3. Vlamsalmander	0.8729
4. Die panorama in my truspieël	0.8704
5. Van roes en amarant	0.8704
6. Tydelose gety	0.868
7. Stillerlewe	0.8664
8. Die lenige liefde	0.8623
9. Diorama	0.8623
10. Ligloop	0.8599
11. Landelik	0.8583
12. Digter wordende	0.8567
13. Groot Verseboek	0.8535
14. Geskrifte van 'n vermiste digter	0.8519
15. Die algebra van nood	0.8511
16. Gode van papier	0.8511
17. Vlerke vir my houteend	0.8503
18. As woorde begin droom, 'n keur	0.848
19. Sonskyf	0.848
20. In die buitenste ruimte	0.8472
21. Kleur kom nooit alleen nie	0.8464
22. Duskant die donker/Before it darkens	0.8426
23. Apostroof	0.8418
24. Die mooiste Afrikaanse Liefdesgedigte	0.8418
25. Duskant die einders	0.8418
26. Die stil middelpunt	0.841
27. Toe dit nog vroeg was	0.841
28. Ruggespraak	0.8403
29. Die aandag van jou oë	0.8395
30. Wat die water onthou	0.8395

The closeness centralities of the 30 poetry books with the highest closeness centralities

This means that these titles are central to the Afrikaans poetry network, having close ties with other highly central publishing houses, critics, and publication platforms.

The twenty publishing houses with the highest closeness centralities are given in the following table:

Publisher	Closeness
1. Protea	0.8551
2. Tafelberg	0.753
3. Human & Rousseau	0.7379
4. Kwêla	0.6841
5. Lapa	0.6771
6. Suider Kollege	0.6426
7. Belmonte	0.6412
8. Bent	0.6342
9. Quillerie	0.6324
10. Homeros	0.6243
11. Genugtig!	0.6163
12. Self publication	0.6078
13. Praag	0.5987
14. Umuzi	0.5971
15. Snailpress	0.5906
16. Hond BK	0.5843
17. Hemel & See	0.5798
18. Cordis trust	0.5791
19. Suikerbos	0.5554
20. Bel Monte	0.5448

The twenty publishing houses with the highest closeness centralities

Again, it can be said that these publishing houses function at the core of the Afrikaans poetry network, with Protea of course scoring the highest. Note also that FAB is absent from this list: As a peripheral publishing house, FAB of course does not have a short path to all other entities – as is also the case with the Kew Gardens example. While in the simple example network entity A scored highest on both betweenness and closeness centrality, the dissimilarity of betweenness and closeness centrality scores in terms of FAB illustrates that there is a large variance between these two centrality measures. 'Importance,' as noted in the discussion of betweenness centrality, is therefore a specific type of importance: Being in a structurally advantageous position to facilitate the introduction of fresh material, like Granovetter's weak ties. This kind of importance does however not necessarily mean influential. FAB's importance in this network simply means that by publishing the works of Floris A. Brown, they add material to the network that would otherwise not have been present.

The twenty publication platforms (periodicals, journals, and websites) with the highest closeness centralities are given in the following table:

Publication platform	Closeness
1. www.litnet.co.za	0.9534
2. Burger	0.9293
3. Beeld	0.9065
4. Literator	0.8967
5. Tydskrif vir Letterkunde	0.8967
6. Rapport	0.895
7. www.versindaba.co.za	0.8924
8. Volksblad	0.8519
9. Stilet	0.8267
10. www.slipnet.co.za	0.7661
11. Current Writing	0.7636
12. Boekeblok	0.7326
13. Fine Music Radio	0.7245
14. Insig	0.7245
15. joanhambidge.blogspot.com	0.7245
16. LitNet Akademies	0.7144
17. Boeke24	0.6826
18. www.vryeafrikaan.co.za	0.6512
19. johanndelange.blogspot.com	0.5869
20. Tydskrif vir Geesteswetenskappe	0.5691

The twenty publication platforms (periodicals, journals, and websites) with the highest closeness centralities

This table suggests that these publication platforms play central roles in contributing to the Afrikaans poetry canon. LitNet's first position should come as no surprise: This website forms a hub where reviews and interviews are published and what Van Wyk Louw called "the open discussion" occurs. However, closeness centrality – like betweenness centrality as discussed above – also indicate an ability to provide a measure of coherence. *Current Writing* may not be a hub of activity as LitNet is, but the journal provides a link with other literary traditions. Also, one cannot help but wonder what the position of *Insig* would have been if this magazine had not closed its doors in 2007: It's fourteenth place is due to its activities from 2000 to 2007, unlike LitNet, which has been active throughout. For five years, this magazine has not contributed to this network at all, and yet it retains a relatively high closeness centrality.

The critics and scholars with the highest closeness centralities are given in the table on the following page.

These are then the critics and scholars that function at the core of the Afrikaans poetry network. Note Joan Hambidge's score of 1: as in the case of betweenness centrality, this is the highest score that can be achieved when centralities are normalized, which means that of all entities – works, poets, critics, publication platforms and publishing houses – Hambidge in her role as critic functions at the absolute core of the poetry network. This also indicates how close Hambidge and Odendaal are: Odendaal scored highest on betweenness centrality, and Hambidge second highest, while these positions are reversed when calculating closeness centrality. Both these critics therefore play a very important role in constructing the poetry canon, and their betweenness- and closeness centrality scores are so close that it becomes impossible to indicate which is more important in terms of network structure.

A micro level approach

Critic	Closeness
1. Hambidge, Joan	1
2. Odendaal, Bernard	0.9978
3. Crous, Marius	0.8889
4. Viljoen, Louise	0.8779
5. Du Plooy, Heilna	0.8655
6. Beukes, Marthinus	0.8575
7. Bezuidenhout, Zandra	0.8449
8. Coetzee, Ampie	0.8449
9. Esterhuizen, Louis	0.8312
10. Naudé, Charl-Pierre	0.8237
11. Cloete, T.T.	0.823
12. Hugo, Daniel	0.8186
13. Olivier, Fanie	0.8057
14. Van Vuuren, Helize	0.8057
15. Visagie, Andries	0.8022
16. De Wet, Karen	0.8001
17. Taljard, Marlies	0.798
18. Malan, Lucas	0.7878
19. Pieterse, H.J.	0.7851
20. Smuts, Lisbé	0.7817
21. Spies, Lina	0.7811
22. Pakendorf, Gunther	0.7784
23. Slippers, Bibi	0.7784
24. Snyman, Henning	0.7784
25. Cochrane, Neil	0.7732
26. Van Wyk, Steward	0.7732
27. Wasserman, Herman	0.7687
28. Myburg, Melt	0.7674
29. John, Philip	0.7655
30. Marais, Johann Lodewyk	0.7585

The critics and scholars with the highest closeness centralities

The poets with the highest closeness centralities are given in the following table:

Poet	Closeness
1. Hambidge, Joan	0.7035
2. Krog, Antjie	0.6934
3. Hugo, Daniel	0.6913
4. De Lange, Johann	0.6862
5. Vos, Cas	0.6781
6. Aucamp, Hennie	0.6756
7. Spies, Lina	0.6721
8. Esterhuizen, Louis	0.6712
9. Olivier, Fanie	0.6712
10. Joubert, Marlise	0.6668
11. Breytenbach, Breyten	0.6663
12. Bekker, Pirow	0.6639
13. Laurie, Trienke	0.6634
14. Grobler, Mari	0.6629
15. Van Rooyen, Piet	0.6629
16. Walters, MM.	0.6629
17. Bosman, Martjie	0.6625
18. Myburg, Melt	0.661
19. Van Niekerk, Dolf	0.6587
20. Gibson, Gilbert	0.6563

The poets with the highest closeness centralities

As poet, Joan Hambidge is again at the top of the list, which suggests that she has played a particularly important role in producing as well as promoting poetry in the contemporary Afrikaans poetry system. Remember that a distinction was made here between people's roles as poets and as critics – as far as Visualizer is concerned, the Joan Hambidge who scored the highest of all critics on closeness centrality and the poet Joan Hambidge are two different and completely unrelated people. The objective of splitting people's roles was precisely to view their contributions separately, but in the case of Hambidge, it can clearly be said that she is *the* central figure in the Afrikaans poetry network.

The above means that these poets, publication platforms, publishing houses and critics and scholars are the most connected to the rest of the network, and thus constitute the center of the forming poetry canon. Full canonization only occurs once they are included in literary histories, but when compiling a literary history, these poets should be considered specifically. Note that all centrality measures indicate *structural positions*: whether these poets are included in literary histories is determined by literary tastes and subjective judgments about the 'quality' of their work, not by their structural positions alone. That said, their structural positions suggest that literary tastes have already singled these poets out as producing 'quality' poetry: Joan Hambidge's and Antjie Krog's positions in the above table suggests above all else that closeness centrality is a useful indicator of literary prestige.

6

Centrality and marginality in the Afrikaans poetry network

As was noted in the discussion of entropy and feedback in terms of non-equilibrium thermodynamics, the core/periphery distinction in the literary system has long been an important feature of a polysystems theory approach to literature. Even-Zohar for instance writes that the literary system is "dominated by its center," which is "identical with the most prestigious canonized repertoire" (Even-Zohar 1990, 89, 17, see also J.H. Senekal 1987, 183). In this view, innovation enters the system from the periphery, and there are perpetual "dynamic tensions between the center and the periphery that guarantee the viability of the cultural system" (Codde 2003, 105), much like an organic system survives through its open relationship with its environment. As such, literary systems import from other literary systems, both in terms of form and content (J. H. Senekal 1987, 171), but also interact with the larger environment in which texts are written and read (see e.g. J.H. Senekal 1987, 169-190 and B.A. Senekal 2012b, 619-620).

In practice also, terms such as "marginal" and "peripheral" are often used to discuss writers and poets in a literary system, along with genres, perspectives, and the like. The September 2010 conference of the Afrikaanse Letterkundige Vereniging (ALV) [Afrikaans Literary Society] had as topic, 'Marginality in literature,' with scholars delivering papers on translations, marginal poets, middle-brow literature, music lyrics, and film – all topics dealing with what these scholars consider to be the periphery of Afrikaans literature. However, it is extremely difficult to *prove* centrality or marginality: Intuition suggests that poets such as Elisabeth Eybers, Antjie Krog, and N.P. van Wyk Louw should be considered canonized and at the core of the Afrikaans literary system, while Wopko Jensma, Hunter Kennedy and Floris A Brown should be peripheral to the Afrikaans poetry network. For the experienced scholar, centrality and marginality are self-evident; no one at this conference suggested any mechanism or criteria to determine whether their topics were suitable or not.

While centrality calculations, which are usually part of a study using SNA, are able to identify the key entities in a network by considering the entire network through a mathematical calculation, it is when the network is represented visually that the use of mathematical graph theory – which underpins much of network theory – comes to fruition. Hoppe and Reinelt (2010, 602) write, "Many networks feature a core/periphery structure. The core is a dominant central cluster, while the periphery has relatively few connections" (see also Boyd et al. 2010, 126). In order to represent the network visually, various layout options are available, including orthogonal, hierarchical, and force-directed, of which the latter is the most popular for scientific enquiry. Various force-directed layout algorithms have been developed since the 1960s, notably those by Eades (1984), Kamada and Kawai (1989), and Fruchterman and Reingold (1991). Of course there are differences between the various force-directed algorithms discussed in for instance Kobourov (2013), Hu (2011) and Di Battista et al. (1994), but most have in common that they consider a network as a physical system (e.g. a mechanical system or atomic particles), where the ties between entities act as forces of attraction and repulsion (Merico, Gfeller, and Bader 2009, 922, Di Battista et al. 1994, 242 Fruchterman and Reingold 1991, 1131). As Suderman and Hallett (2007, 2654) write, force-directed layouts "are also known as spring embeddings since edges [ties] are modeled as springs that pull linked nodes together, or push unlinked nodes apart, until the layout reaches a state of equilibrium." Notably, when calculating these physical forces in a network, these algorithms take *every* entity and relationship into account – of course there cannot be a core without entities acting on the periphery. In addition, these calculations are made using the information contained in the graph itself, i.e. using relationship data, and not on other "domain-specific knowledge" (Kobourov 2013, 383). For instance, in the literary network, calculations are not made using the perceived importance of scholars, critics and authors, but rather using the ties between these role players. Force-directed algorithms are still evolving, and like network theory in general, have multidisciplinary applications (Kobourov 2013, 403): all the network visualizations provided throughout this book have been done with force-directed layout algorithms.

Using a force-directed layout, those entities with the best connections (not necessarily the highest number of connections) are positioned at the core of the network, while those with few or few strategically significant connections are positioned at the periphery. In Senekal (2013d), it is for instance shown that while the Afrikaans poet Floris A. Brown has a large number of connections (because of his high number of publications), he is still positioned at the periphery of the Afrikaans poetry network – *where* connections lead are more important in a force-directed layout than the number of connections by themselves. A position at the center of the network – as is the case in various versions of systems theory, including polysystem theory – then suggests importance in a network, as Kobourov (2013, 397) writes, "in traditional drawings in R^2 [two-dimensional Euclidean space] there is an implicit assumption that nodes in the center are important, while nodes on the periphery are less important". It follows that in addition to the abovementioned centrality calculations, force-directed layouts of systems can identify the important entities in a system.

The use of mathematics in providing the layout of a network is crucial in being able to position entities objectively, as Merico, Gfeller, and Bader (2009, 923) write, "Networks are well-defined mathematical objects. Thus, analysis patterns can be implemented computationally, enabling automated and unbiased hypothesis generation". The result of a network visualization with a force-directed layout is thus entirely replicable by any researcher, and what this means in practice, is that an entity's position as peripheral or at the core can be measured without literary tastes, personal views or the like having an effect on the analysis.

In the previous chapter, it was mentioned that closeness centrality is also a measure of overall centrality, since entities that are on average closer to other entities are necessarily at the center of the network. This can clearly be seen when the network is visualized

104   *Canons and Connections*

using a force-directed layout. In the following graph, entities with a high closeness centrality score are shown in darker colors (the darker, the higher the closeness centrality):

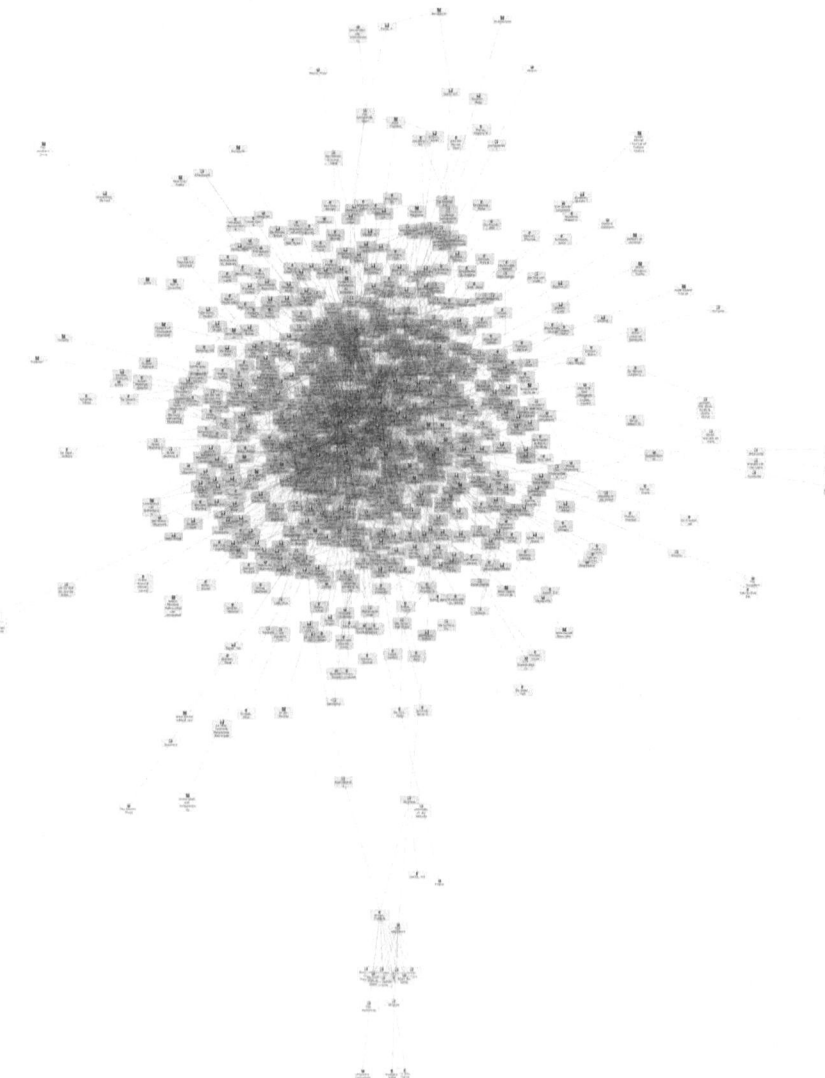

Closeness centrality in the Afrikaans poetry network 2000-2012

Centrality and marginality 105

Clearly, those entities with the highest closeness centrality scores are positioned at the core of the network, while those with low closeness centrality scores are positioned at the periphery. While closeness centrality and a force-directed layout are not identical, there is a very high degree of overlap between these two ways of measuring centrality.

As done throughout this book, it is more sensible to indicate centrality in terms of entity type. The following publication platforms can be found at the center of the network (in no particular order):

1. Insig
2. joanhambidgeblogspot
3. Volksblad
4. www.slipnet.co.za
5. www.litnet.co.za
6. www.versindaba.co.za
7. Burger
8. Beeld
9. Tydskrif vir Letterkunde
10. Literator
11. LitNet Akademies
12. Stilet
13. Rapport

These publication platforms are indicated in the sociogram on the following page by using the above numbers.

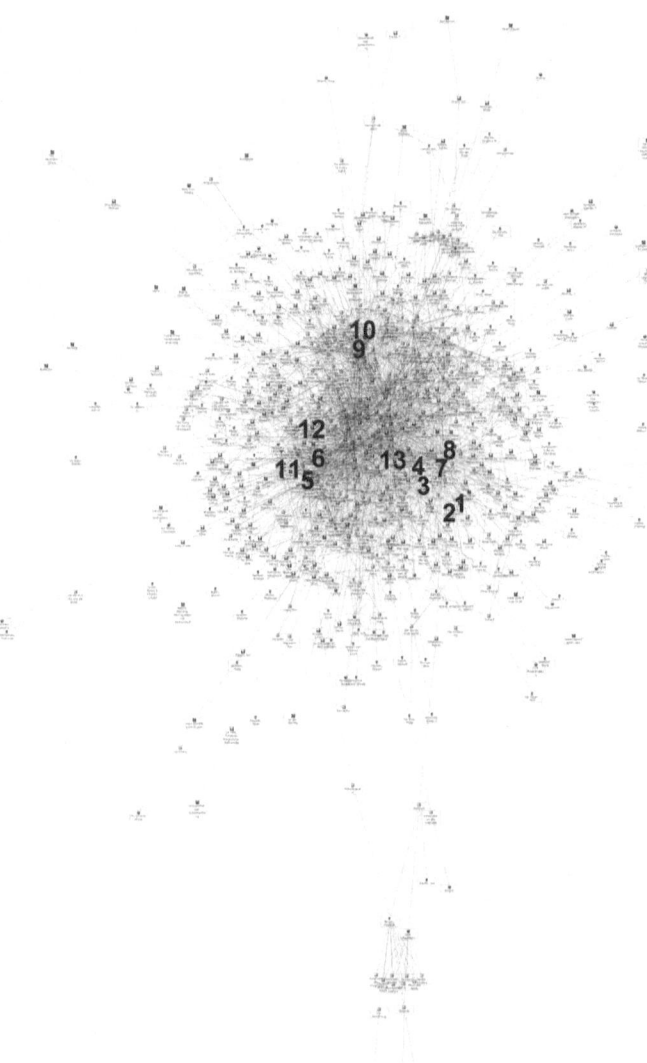

The central publication platforms

The following publishers can be found in the center of this network:
1. Kwêla
2. Human & Rousseau
3. Lapa

4. Tafelberg
5. Protea

These publishers are indicated in the following sociogram using the above numbers:

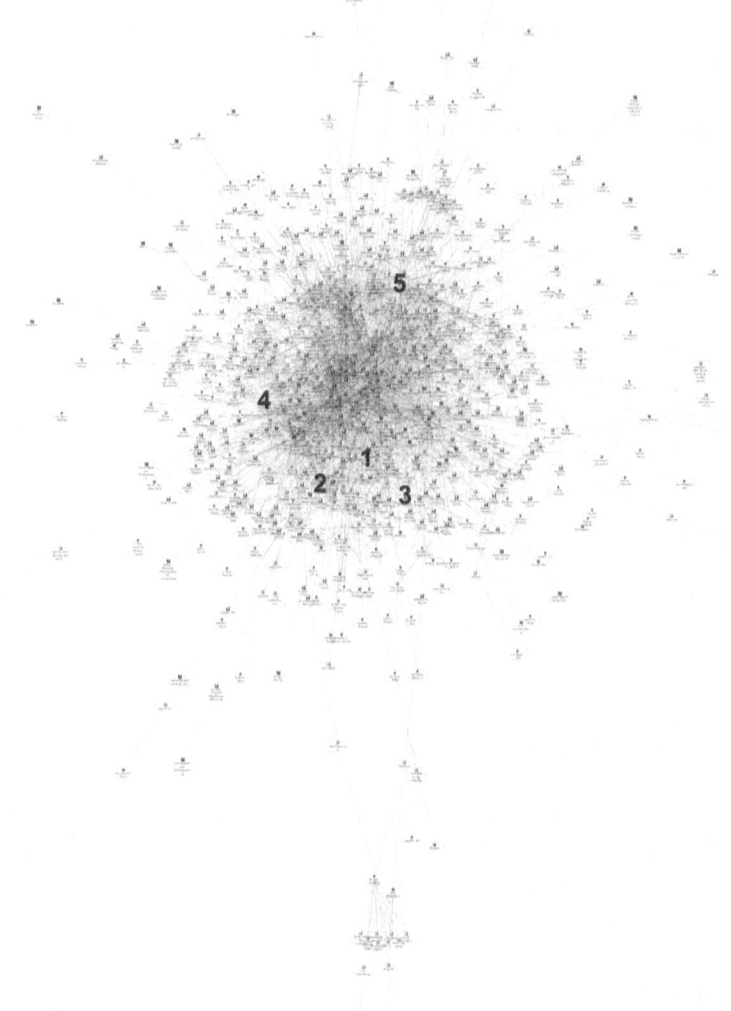

The central publishing houses

Publishing houses therefore function slightly further away from the core than publication platforms. I suspect this may be the result of the density of the core that provides a great variety of ties between entities in the core, making publishing houses slightly less central. Because these are nevertheless crucial entities in the literary system, their positions suggest that the core may have to be drawn in such a way that it includes them.

Some of the critics that play a central role are the following (in no particular order):

1. Bernard Odendaal
2. Joan Hambidge
3. Marius Crous
4. Louise Viljoen
5. Heilna du Plooy
6. T.T. Cloete
7. Hennie Aucamp
8. Helize van Vuuren
9. André P. Brink
10. Marthinus Beukes

These critics are again indicated in the sociogram on the following page.

These are however only ten of the critics that function at the center, while many more are positioned around them. The following list shows *all* the critics that can be extracted from the center (in alphabetical order):

- Anker, Willem
- Aucamp, Hennie

Centrality and marginality 109

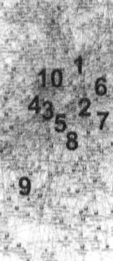

Some of the central critics

- Bennett, Nini
- Beukes, Marthinus
- Bezuidenhout, Zandra
- Britz, Elretha
- Britz, Etienne
- Cilliers, Stefnie
- Cloete, T.T.
- Cochrane, Neil
- Coetzee, Ampie
- Crous, Marius
- De Beer, A.M.
- De Goede, Ronel
- De Lange, Johann
- De Villiers, Helene
- De Vries, Willem
- De Wet, Karen
- Du Plessis, Leané
- Du Plooy, Heilna
- Ester, Hans
- Esterhuizen, Louis
- Gaigher, Louis
- Gouws, Tom
- Grové, A.P.
- Hambidge, Joan
- Hugo, Daniel
- John, Philip
- Kannemeyer, J.C.
- Lourens, Amanda
- Malan, Lucas
- Muller, Petra
- Myburg, Johan
- Myburg, Melt
- Naudé, Charl-Pierre
- Nel, Adele
- Nieuwoudt, Stephanie
- Odendaal, Bernard
- Olivier, Fanie
- Pakendorf, Gunther
- Pienaar, Hans
- Pieterse, H.J.
- Roux, Alwyn
- Roux, J.B.
- Schaffer, Alfred
- Slippers, Bibi
- Smith, Francois
- Smuts, Lisbé

Centrality and marginality   111

- Snyman, Henning
- Spies, Lina
- Steinmair, Deborah
- Taljard, Marlies
- Van Coller, H.P
- Van der Westhuizen, Chris
- Van Niekerk, Annemarie
- Van Niekerk, Jacomien
- Van Vuuren, Helize
- Van Wyk, Steward
- Van Zyl, Wium
- Viljoen, Hein
- Viljoen, Louise
- Visagie, Andries
- Vos, Cas
- Walters, M.M.
- Wasserman, Herman

Of course, the texts that function at the center are also important, but again there are a large number of texts at the center. In fact, there are so many texts at the center (because of course the poetry network revolves around poetry publications), that these are listed in Appendix A.

As stated in the introduction, every book published, publisher, poet, critic, and publication do play a role in the literary system, even if their contribution is considered 'marginal', or literary tastes dictate that their contribution is inferior. An important contribution made by the abovementioned conference is that it acknowledged the roles played by the marginal. 'Marginal' is something different from 'negligible', and hence, the following graph shows some of the works that can be found on the periphery of this network (all published music lyrics):

1. *Woorde* (Fokofpolisiekar)
2. *Toorwoorde roep my* (Valient Swart)
3. *Hitte vannie teerpad* (Anton Goosen)
4. *Heuning in die mond* (Jak de Priester)

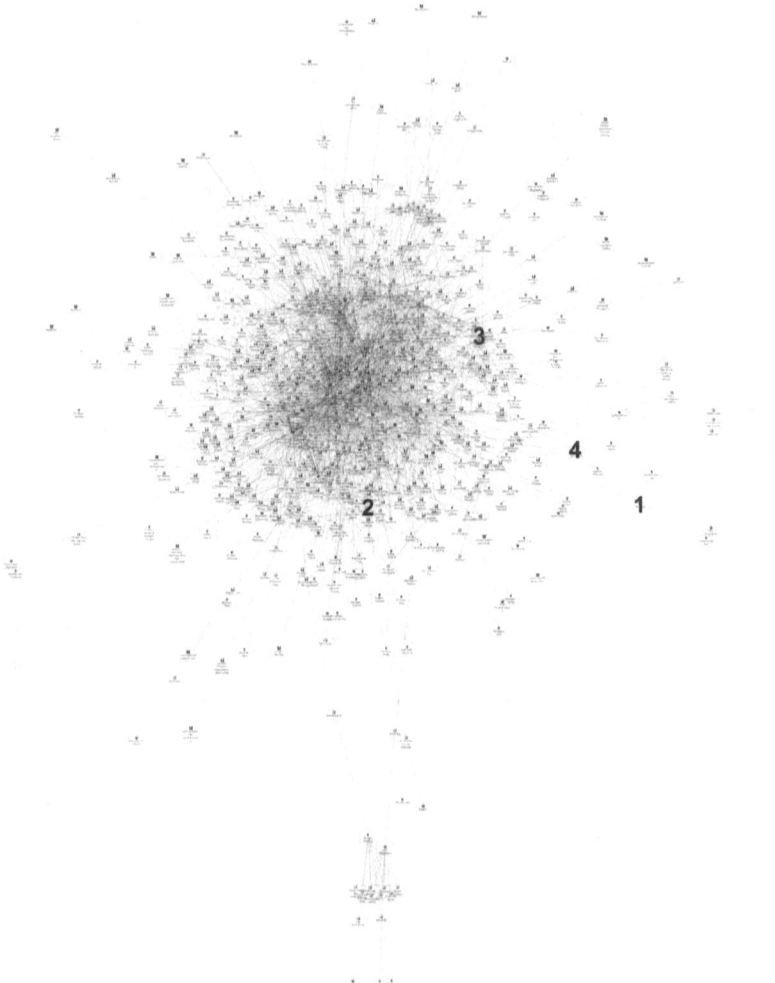

The positions of published lyrics in the network

Here it can clearly be seen that music lyrics are peripheral to the Afrikaans poetry network. While some scholars advocate the study of central authors in a literary system, one could also argue for the study of these marginal figures, because while a lot has been written on central poets (hence their centrality), little has been written on those on the periphery. The above does not suggest who should be studied; rather it shows who *has been* studied, and who has not. Future studies can continue to focus on the central poets, but an-

Centrality and marginality   113

other way to use the above centrality is to identify those poets who have been studied very little, and may warrant special attention.

The question is of course: *Why* are some works central in this layout, while others are peripheral. In a network, well-connected entities are positioned at the center, and hence the works that were written about by the most important (in a structural sense) critics will be positioned at the center. Take for instance Heilna du Plooy's book of poetry, *In die landskap ingelyf,* whose position is indicated with an X:

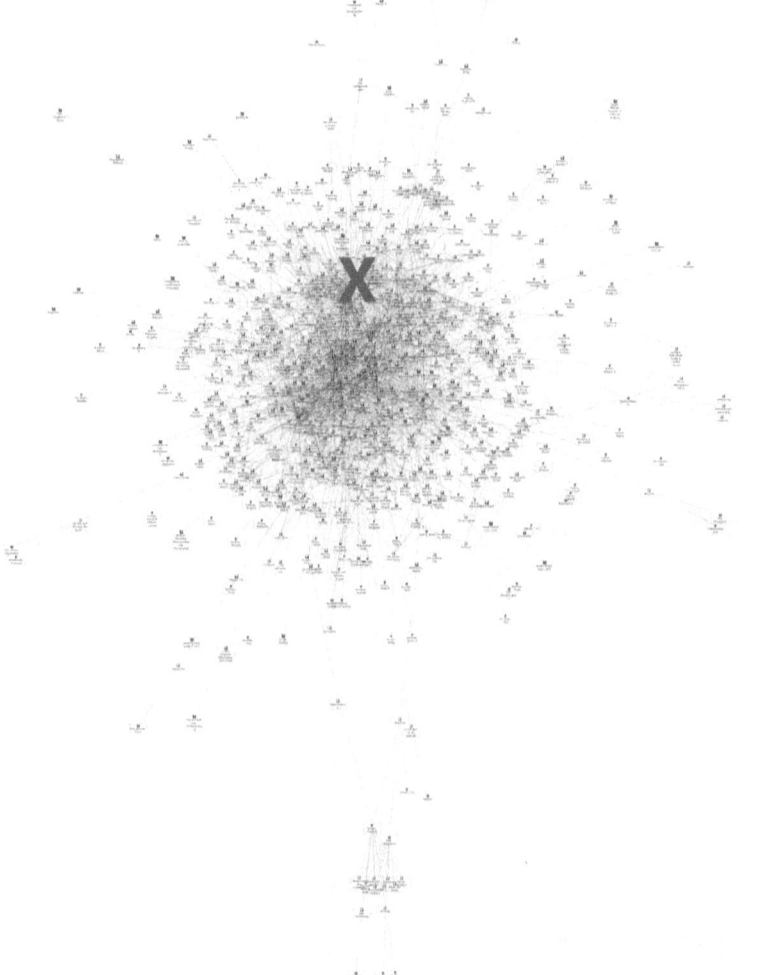

In die landskap ingelyf's *position in the network*

114 *Canons and Connections*

This work was published at Protea, which has been shown to be the dominant publishing house in terms of Afrikaans poetry. Protea achieved this status through its overall publications; the following are the poets that published through this publishing house:

- Aucamp, Hennie
- Bekker, Pirow
- Belcher, Ronnie
- Bezuidenhout, Andries
- Bezuidenhout, Zandra
- Bosman, Martjie
- Crous, Marius
- De Coninck, Herman
- De Kock, Leon
- De Lange, Johann
- De Wette, Julian
- Deacon, Thomas
- Dönges, Sarina
- Du Plessis, Phil
- Du Plooy, Heilna
- Esterhuizen, Louis
- Goosen, Anton
- Grobbelaar, Pieter
- Grobler, Mari
- Hambidge Joan
- Henderson, WJ.
- Hugo, Daniel
- Jonckheere, Wilfred
- Joubert, Marlise
- Kombuis, Koos
- Kopland, Rutger
- Laurie, Trienke
- Lombard, Chris
- Lombard, Kobus
- Malan, Lucas
- Marais, Eugène N.
- Marais, Johann Lodewyk
- Möller, Lucie
- Myburg, Melt
- Naudé, Charl-Pierre
- Olivier, Fanie
- Philander, PJ.
- Phillips, Fransi
- Pieterse, HJ
- Pretorius, Wessel

Centrality and marginality   115

- Rainer, Maria Rilke
- Rall, Henk
- Smit, Rosa
- Snyders, Peter
- Spies, Lina
- Toerien, Barend
- Van Hee, Miriam
- Van Jerusalem, Johannes
- Van Niekerk, Dolf
- Van Rooyen, Piet
- Viljoen, Hein
- Vos, Cas
- Walters, MM.
- Weideman, George
- Wierenga, Jelleke

On this list, one can see the names of many established poets, including Hennie Aucamp, Pirow Bekker, Joan Hambidge, Daniel Hugo, Marlise Joubert, Koos Kombuis, Eugene Marais, Lina Spies, Barend Toerien, M.M. Walters, and George Weideman. Through publishing the works of these acclaimed poets, Protea gains literary prestige, which then reflects upon the rest of the poets on its publishing list. It is no accident that Anton Goosen's work of poetry is closer to the center in the above figure than Fokofpolisiekar's *Woorde*: Goosen published at *the* publishing house of the poetry network. The publishing house is then the first entity type that draws Heilna du Plooy's work closer to the center.

Secondly, *In die landskap ingelyf* was reviewed by Bernard Odendaal, Lucas Malan and Philip John. As we have seen, Bernard Odendaal (together with Joan Hambidge) is the dominant literary critic, and by paying attention to Du Plooy's work, he then draws the work closer to the center. Philip John and Lucas Malan are also important critics, which again contributes to *In die landskap ingelyf*'s position.

Similarly, we have seen that Joan Hambidge is the poet with the highest closeness centrality. She also published at Protea, but she published a lot more widely than Heilna du Plooy, including at Tafelberg and at Human & Rousseau. Her publishing history alone therefore draws her closer to the center, but consider which critics reviewed her work:

116   *Canons and Connections*

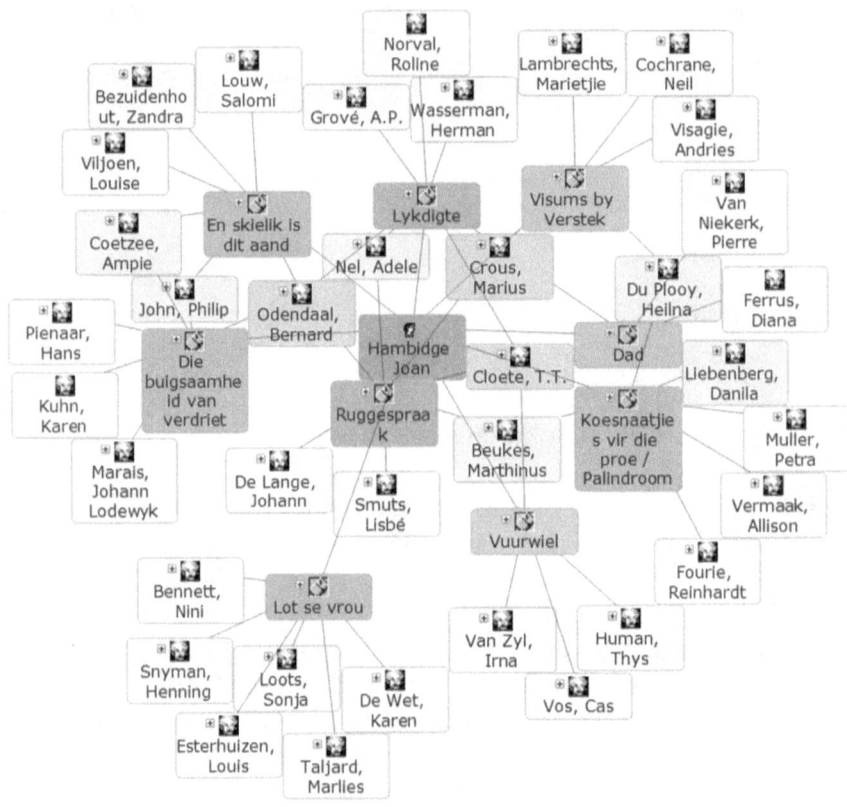

Joan Hambidge's critics

Among these are Bernard Odendaal, T.T. Cloete, Marius Crous, Marthinus Beukes, Heilna du Plooy, Marlies Taljard, Louis Esterhuizen, and other important critics. When the positions of her works are plotted in the entire network, it can be seen that all of them occupy central positions in the network:

1. *Lot se vrou*

2. *Vuurwiel*

3. *Ruggespraak*

4. *Koesnaatjies vir die proe*

Centrality and marginality 117

5. *Die buigsaamheid van verdriet*
6. *En skielik is dit aand*
7. *Lykdigte*
8. *Visums by verstek*

The positions of Hambidge's works

Compare Hambidge's publishing context with those of the marginal lyrics writers:

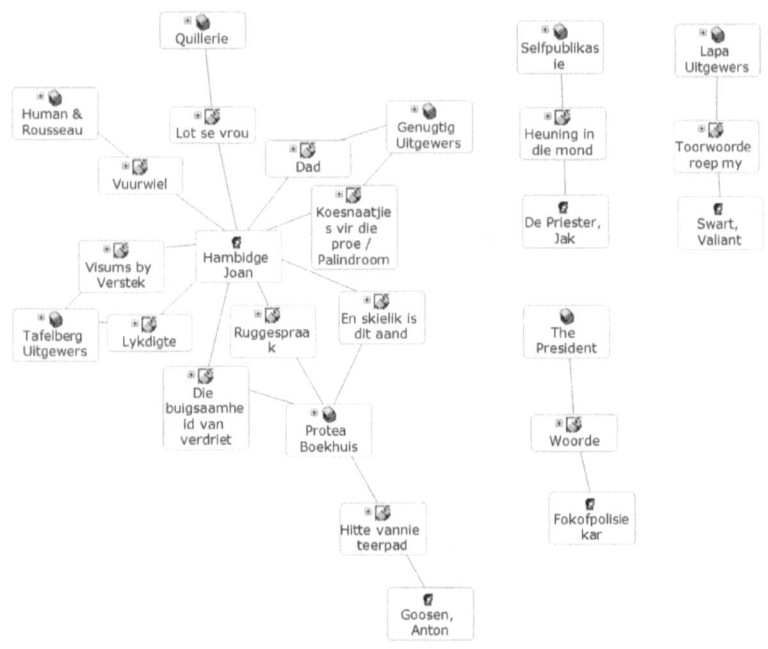

Hambidge and the lyrics writers, publishers

While Hambidge publishes at renowned publishing houses, and indeed the publishing houses with the highest closeness centralities, De Priester self-published his work, and Fokofpolisiekar used an otherwise unknown publisher. Goosen also published at Protea, but he only published one anthology, and only at Protea. When critics are considered, the difference between her and the lyrics writers is even more stark, with none of the critics who review Hambidge's work reviewing those of the musicians (although Hambidge herself reviewed Valiant Swart's work).

Perhaps it would be illuminating not to compare Hambidge with marginal poets, but rather central ones. In the closeness centrality calculation, it was shown that Joan Hambidge is the poet with the highest closeness centrality followed by Antjie Krog. Because Krog was indicated as the most-studied poet, this raises the question: Why would Hambidge be more central than Krog? The first part of the answer concerns publishers: While Hambidge published at Protea, Tafelberg, Human & Rousseau, Quillerie, and Genugtig!, Krog published at Kwêla, Umuzi, Tafelberg, and Human & Rousseau, but not at Protea. By publishing at the dominant publisher, Hambidge is already drawn closer to the core of the network. But the real difference comes in when critics are compared: While Bernard Odendaal, Heilna du Plooy, Marthinus Beukes, Andries Visagie, Louise Viljoen and Louis Esterhuizen publish on both poets, important critics are absent in Krog's connections, including Marius Crous, Cas Vos, Johann Lodewyk Marais, Philip John, Ampie Coetzee, Salomi Louw, Zandra Bezuidenhout, Nini Bennett, and A.P. Grové. The slight difference in publishing context, along with this review context, places Hambidge in a slightly more central position using a closeness centrality calculation. When their positions are indicated on a graph, however, the difference is no longer slight (Hambidge = 1, Krog = 2):

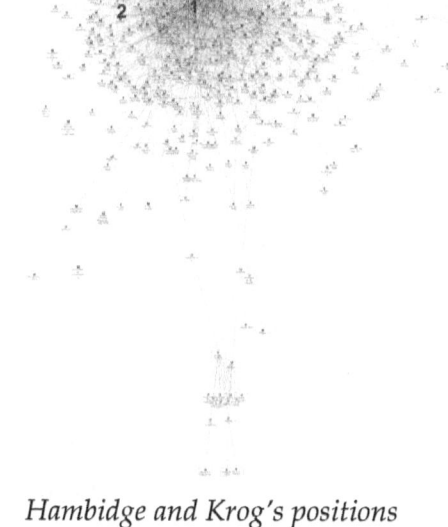

Hambidge and Krog's positions

Of course, this does not imply that Hambidge's poetry is 'better' than Krog's: all the above indicates is that Hambidge has better connections than Krog.

Let us consider another example and from a different angle: Gilbert Gibson, who published four works of poetry in this period:

1. boomplaats
2. oogensiklopedie
3. kaplyn
4. vii

These works can be found in the following positions:

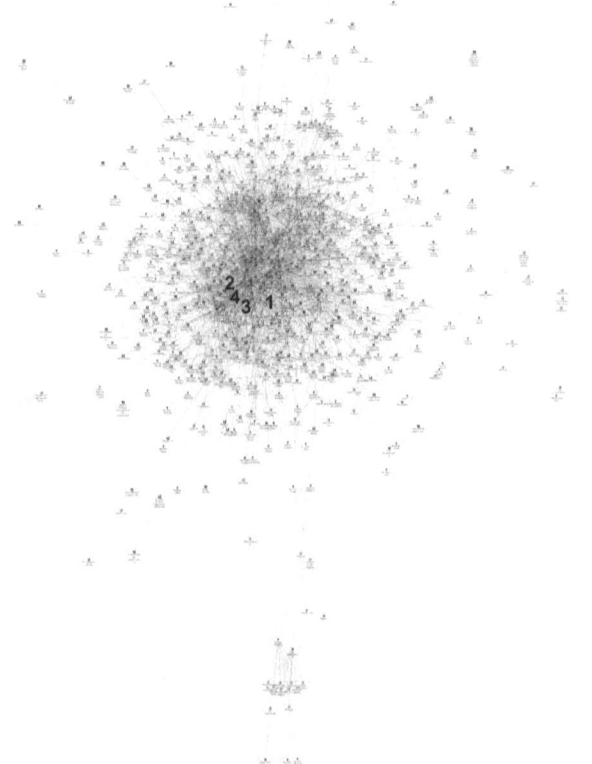

Gibson's works in the network

Centrality and marginality 121

All four his publications are therefore highly central to the network. Firstly, all four were published at Tafelberg – one of the dominant publishing houses in this network – and hence, Gibson's works should already be drawn towards the core. Furthermore, Bernard Odendaal reviewed *Boomplaats* and *Oogensiklopedie*, while the latter was also reviewed by Joan Hambidge, who also reviewed a second work of Gibson's, *Kaplyn*. Other reviewers who reviewed more than one of Gibson's works include Zandra Bezuidenhout, Ampie Coetzee, Charl-Pierre Naudé, Marthinus Beukes and Louise Viljoen – all critics that have consistently scored high on all centrality measures. Gibson's second-degree connections (entities connected to his publications) are therefore important role players in the network. When their connections are considered, in other words Gibson's third degree connections, it can be seen how well connected Gibson is through these entities:

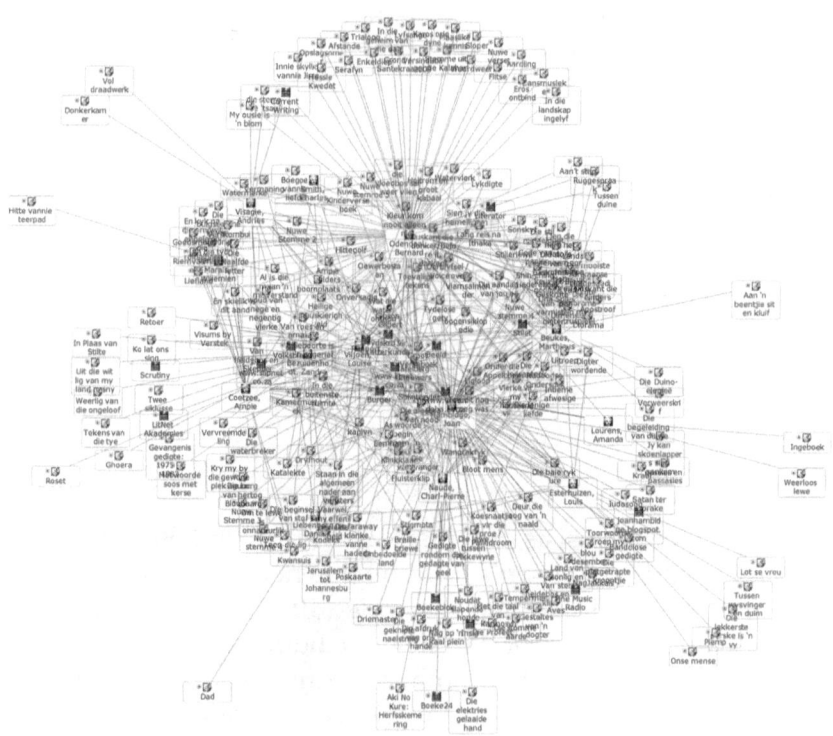

Gibson's third degree connections

Because those critics who paid attention to Gibson's works are some of the best-connected critics in the entire network, and because he published at one of the dominant publishers, his third degree connections already span 220 entities with 462 connections. This means that some of the most active role players have devoted attention to his works, contributing to his works' overall position at the very core of the network. Now consider Floris A. Brown's third degree network:

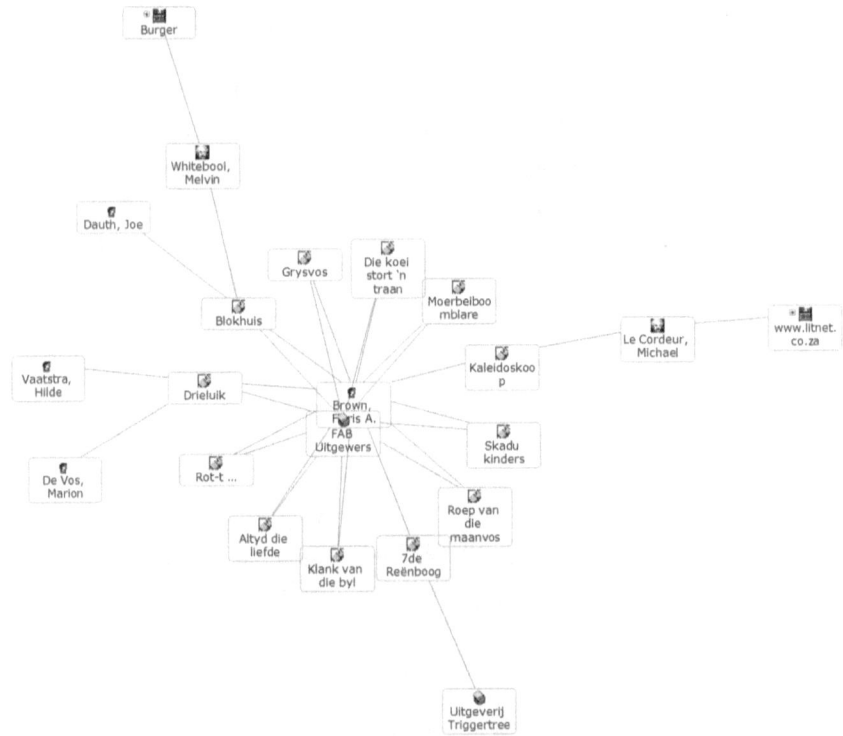

Brown's third degree connections

This network consists of a mere 22 entities and 30 connections – literally a tenth of Gibson's third degree network. The difference lies in both the publisher and the critics: Brown was published by FAB and Uitgeverij Triggertree, who are both marginal publishers. In addition, not one of the dominant critics paid attention to his works, and the result is that his works can be found in the following positions:

Centrality and marginality 123

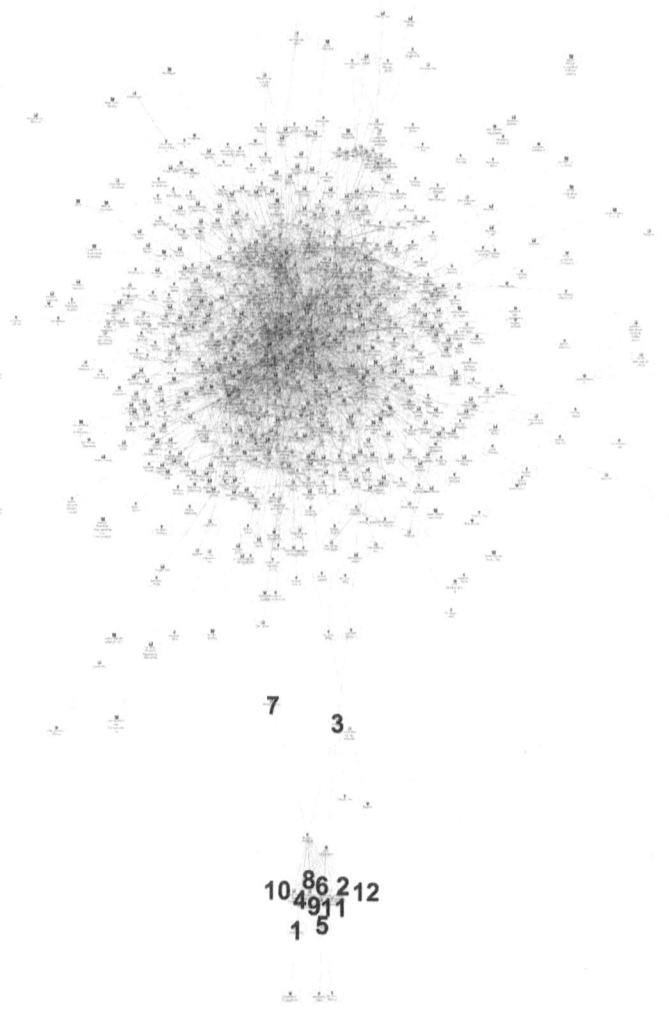

Brown's works in the poetry network

Key:

1. *7de Reënboog*
2. *Altyd die liefde*
3. *Blokhuis*

4. *Die koei stort 'n traan*

5. *Drieluik*

6. *Grysvos*

7. *Kaleidoskoop*

8. *Klank van die byl*

9. *Moerbeiboomblare*

10. *Roep van die maanvos*

11. *Rot-t ...*

12. *Skadu kinders*

Of course this is not to imply that Gibson is a 'better' poet than Brown – judgments of quality, as I have said, are better left to the critics. What this example does illustrate, however, is that in terms of the poetry system, Gibson's works are central, while Brown's works are not.

The same could be done with any poet. Three degrees from Hambidge shows a network consisting of 281 entities, while three degrees from Antjie Krog results in a network of 271, indicating the difference made by slightly disparate review and publishing contexts that result in Hambidge's higher closeness centrality.

From the above examples, it can be seen how the literary system functions: *who* reviews a poet's works and *where* these works were published determines whether a work is ultimately positioned at the core or on the periphery of the network. However, these second-degree connections are not decisive in themselves: Whose works the publisher also published, and whose works a reviewer also reviewed, come into play. Overall, centrality does not even stop here: Centrality is based on where connections of connections of connections of connections lead, with each entity gathering importance and transferring that prestige onto his connections, which then influences their connections, and so forth. In the end, a position at the core is the result of *all* 1834 connections in the network: every publication and every review or study ultimately has bearing on an entity's position.

As noted earlier, it has long been alleged that a position in the canon is dependent on among others these role players, and that works that are not reviewed or studied by the right people cannot be regarded as literature (J. H. Senekal 1987, 178). What the above illustrates is that the same applies to positioning in the network as done through a force-directed layout algorithm. There are, however, two major differences between claims made in the past within the polysystem framework, and claims made here.

Firstly, the network is concrete in the above analysis, not an abstract conception of a system. The system is treated as a physical system with forces acting upon entities, and it can clearly be seen what is found in the center and what can be found on the periphery. As such, the literary system has not been studied in such a concrete way.

Secondly, positions at the core or periphery cannot be influenced by the researcher's own literary tastes. The network is a binary object in the sense that a connection is present, or it is not. When care is taken to include all connections, the network is treated as a physical object and personal views do not enter into positioning an entity at the core or on the periphery: this investigation is entirely replicable by any researcher, regardless of personal tastes. As such, it offers a scientific way to determine whether a work of poetry is central or peripheral.

There is, however, one significant problem that remains: Where is the boundary between the core and the periphery? While Gibson's works are clearly at the core, and Brown's works are clearly on the periphery, how about a work such as Hennie Aucamp's *Hittegolf*, which is indicated with an X in the graph on the following page.

Is this position at the core, or on the periphery? While for many works, positions are clearly seen in a visualization, the distinction between core and periphery becomes problematic when boundary cases are involved. One way to resolve the issue would be to include a third category, semi-core/semi-periphery, but that creates an additional boundary that also needs to be defined. It would be possible to take the third of entities with the highest closeness centralities and call that the core, while the third with the lowest closeness centralities would then be the periphery, and the remaining third could then be called the semi-core/semi-periphery. Such

126   *Canons and Connections*

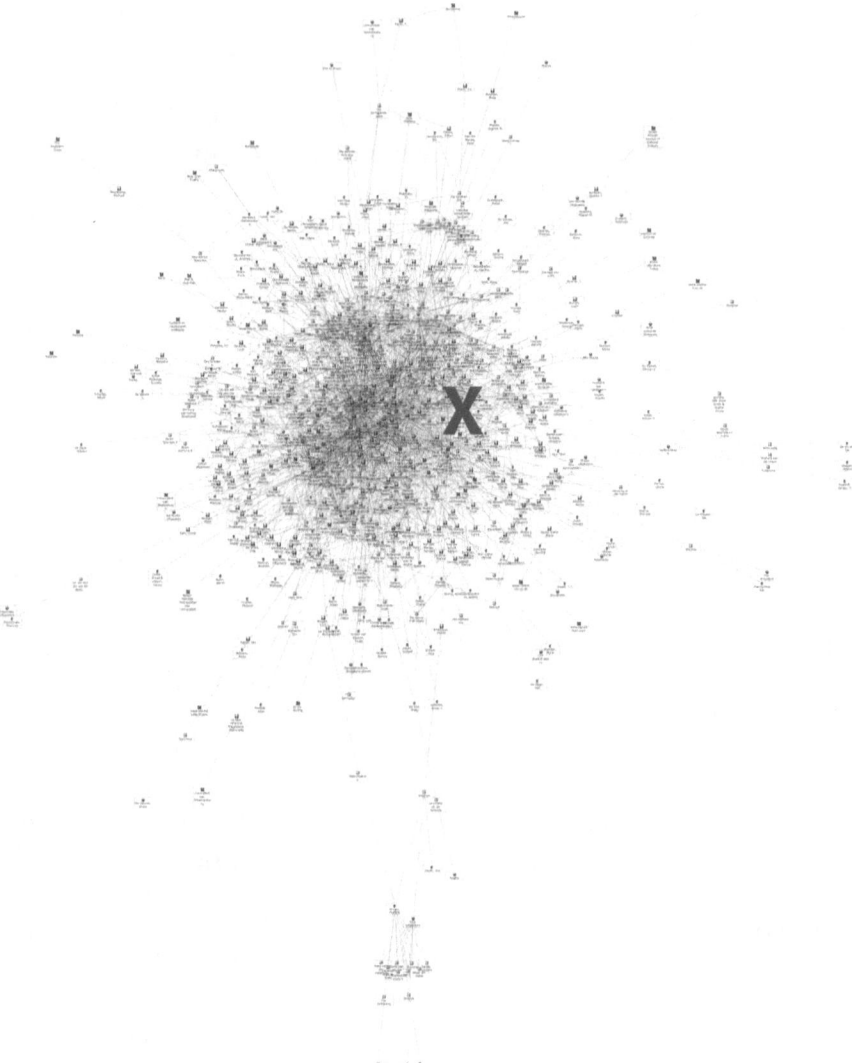

Hittegolf *in the poetry network*

a distinction may be precise, but it seems overly arbitrary to classify a work as semi-core rather than core when the difference could well be 0.0001 of a closeness centrality calculation. Similarly, merely defining the very center of the network with a force-directed algorithm is problematic; how far away from this center would the boundary of the core be? Further research and debate will be required to resolve this issue.

Regardless of the latter, the use of a force-directed layout algorithm and the closeness centrality calculation can be an important step towards finding an objective way with which to classify authors and works. While it is impossible to determine where the boundary between core and periphery lies, the works that are clearly on the periphery could be specially selected for study, as could those that are clearly positioned at the core. This could provide a scientific basis for the abovementioned conference on marginality in literature, or a special issue of a literary journal, while the selection of authors for a literary history could similarly focus on authors and texts identified as belonging to the core. The important conclusion one can make from this chapter is although some finer details remain unresolved, this method does provide a scientific starting point for numerous future applications.

7

Conclusion

In a short interview on SABC2's news in 2011, I noted that digital source documents not only help us preserve our heritage, but it also allows us to take a fresh look at our existing data. In the publication on information technology for research purposes that followed the Heritage Foundation-funded project, I reiterated the same sentiments. Network theory is currently one of the foremost ways in which man and machine have developed a synergy in a research environment, and the result has been new discoveries about how the human environment functions.

One thing that almost characterizes network theory is the optimism with which it is employed. In the introduction, Steven Strogatz's (2004[2003], 232) belief that network theory could contribute to understanding life and consciousness was mentioned, and the Committee on Network Science for Future Army Applications shares this enthusiasm, noting, "[H]uman understanding of networks has the potential to play a vital role in the 21st century, which is witnessing the rise of the Connected Age" (Committee on Network Science for Future Army Applications 2005, 18). This enthusiasm was voiced over thirty years ago by Boissevain (1979, 393) when he predicted, "Network analysis has an important future," and discoveries made over the past fifteen years seem to realize his prediction.

This study has taken a new look at the literary network from the perspective of network theory. It was shown how the literary network shares important topological features with other complex networks, which is interesting in itself. The universality of network topology however goes beyond a simple curiosity: it was shown that through the power law degree distribution pattern, it can be proven that the literary system is a self-organizing system. Of course, agents in social systems (people) make their own decisions, but as a whole, decisions about what is considered 'literature' are made within the system itself. No single entity can be responsible for a poet's position in the center of the network: it is through the combined efforts of all role players that works become central or peripheral in the literary system.

One of the crucial implications of the literary network's shared topology with other complex networks is that it opens up the possibility of using discoveries made in other disciplines to interpret how the literary system functions. It was shown how the Matthew Effect in particular might guide the accumulation of literary prestige, and the theory of complex networks has a vast array of theoretical concepts that could aid our understanding of the literary system. Over thirty years ago, Anthony Wilden (1980, 241) wrote, "in such a complex epistemological reorganization as we are experiencing in this century, the new territory staked out by any one discipline, science, or movement cannot be comprehended except in relation to all the others." It is my hope that the suggestions and findings of this book will lead to a broadening of literary theory to also include complexity and networks.

At the node level, the book has discussed whom the key players are in the contemporary Afrikaans poetry network, based on degree-, betweenness-, and closeness centrality. In itself, these findings are hopefully useful: It for instance offers an historical record of who were the most active and who contributed the most new information to the system, as well as who functioned at the core of the network. One could add further classes of role players, and for instance consider which poets are prescribed at which universities, which universities employ the most active scholars, etcetera. Furthermore, one could introduce content to the network: *what* do poets write about, and which other poets write about the same themes? As I am writing this book, a project is already underway that looks at the relationships between poets and painters, asking *whose* paintings inspire *which* poets. The possibilities are endless, and network theory in particular allows the researcher to work not only in a scientifically sound methodology, but also in a highly creative one. Some of the major discoveries in network theory, including those by Euler, Moreno, Milgram, Watts and Strogatz and Barabási and Albert were highly creative undertakings, and apart from network theory's interdisciplinary applications, *creative* applications also characterize network theory. Future research could bring the vibrancy of this method into literary studies.

Of particular importance is the ways of measuring overall network centrality, as measured with closeness centrality and a force-directed layout of the network. Up until now, terms such as 'centrality' and 'marginality' have been used without any scientific basis, and it was shown here, as well as in previous publications, how network theory could be employed to identify the core and periphery of the literary system. This of course leaves the question as to where the boundary between core and periphery actually is – an issue that still needs clarification – but this is already a start. I wrote elsewhere (2013d),

> Network analysis as employed here can be an important step towards conducting the study of the literary system more scientifically. But it also has broader implications: When a conference is organized on marginality in poetry, how are the poets chosen who are labeled as marginal? When a compilation of Afrikaans poetry is published, or a book such as *Perspektief en Profiel*, how is one to decide which poets are to be included and which ones are not? When a special edition of a journal on Afrikaans poetry is planned, who should be the editor? Network theory provides a scientific basis for such decisions.[36]

I have only scratched the surface of network theory's applications in literary studies, and a lot remains to be done. Current projects include an attempt to map the entire Afrikaans literary system from 1900 to 1978. This project should provide the data that would facilitate a longitudinal study, and moreover, it would highlight features that are unique to the poetry network, since works of drama and prose are also considered. A preliminary analysis for instance showed that self-publications are not unique to the contemporary poetry network, as these play an important role in earlier periods as well. The self-publications discussed in this book are therefore not the result of technologies such as print-on-demand and the wider availability of word processing software and computers; self-publication is not unique to the digital world. What *is* unique to poetry, however, is the very existence of self-publications: These are not found in drama or prose.

While these and other projects take a quantitative approach, it is also my hope that my findings will lead to further qualitative studies that examine the literary network in more depth. Network theory provides the theoretical concepts and technical tools to study the literary system on a much broader scale than other methods, but qualitative methods provide more depth, and no doubt contribute significantly to our understanding of how this system functions. The method employed here is new, but it is not intended to supplant any other methodology: In the interest of emergence, I hope that my research can connect to the scientific field of literary studies and our understanding of canonicity.

Appendix A

These are the works of poetry that can be extracted from the center of the network:

[]en die here het foto's geneem oor vanderbijlpark]
Aan 'n beentjie sit en kluif
Afstande
Aki No Kure: Herfsskemering
Al is die maan 'n misverstand
Amper elders
Apostroof
As woorde begin droom, 'n keur
Aves
Bloot mens
Boegoe vannie liefde
boomplaats
Braille-briewe
Dansmusieke
Die aandag van jou oë
Die afdruk van ons hande
Die algebra van nood
Die begeleiding van duiwe
Die beginsel van stof
Die buigsaamheid van verdriet
Die Duino-elegieë
Die geknipte naelstring
Die lenige liefde
Die lewe tussen Pikkewyne

Appendix A

Die mooiste Afrikaanse Liefdesgedigte
Die panorama in my truspieël
Die platgetrapte kroontjie
Die skyn van tuiskoms: 'n keur uit die gedigte van Lina
die sterre sê 'tsau'
Die stil middelpunt
Die twaalfde letter
Die windvanger
Digter wordende
Diorama
Driemaster
Dryfhout
Duskant die donker/Before it darkens
Duskant die einders
Een hart
En skielik is dit aand
Enkeldiep
Fluisterklip
Gedigte rondom die gedagte van geel
Geskrifte van 'n vermiste digter
Ghoera
Goedsmoeds
Grond / Santekraam
Groot Verseboek
Heilige nuuskierigheid
Hittegolf
Holtrom en groot kabaal
In die buitenste ruimte
In die geheim van die dag
In die landskap ingelyf
In die tyd van uile
Innie skylte vannie Jirre
Intieme afwesige
Ja!
Judasoog
Jy kan skoenlappers sien aankom
Kamermusiek
kaplyn

Appendix A 135

Karos orie dyne
Katalekte
Kleur kom nooit alleen nie
Kraai
Land van sonlig en sterre
Landelik
Lang reis na Ithaka
Liefland
Ligloop
Lot se vrou
Lyfsange
Lykdigte
Met die taal van karmosyn
Met woorde soos met kerse
My lied van die niet
Nadoodse Ondersoek
Nag op 'n kaal plein
NagJakkals
Noudat slapende honde
Nuwe stemme 4
Nuwe verset
Oewerbestaan
Om te onthou
Onbedoelde land
Onder die Appelboom
Onversadig
oogensiklopedie
Oorblyfsel / Voice over
Opslagsomer
passies en passasies
Plaaslike kennis
Retoer
Ruggespraak
Satan ter sprake
Shih-ching: Liedereboek
Sien jy die hemelliggame
Sloper
Sonskyf

Spies
Splintervlerk
Staan in die algemeen nader aan vensters
Stigmata
Stillerlewe
Teen die lig
Toe dit nog vroeg was
Toevallige tekens
Tussen wysvinger en duim
Tydelose gety
Uitroep
Vaarwel, my effens bevlekte held
Van heidebos en Skepper
Van roes en amarant
Vermaning
Versindaba 2009
Versindaba 2010
Verweerskrif
vii
Visums by Verstek
Vlamsalmander
Vlerke vir my houteend
Vol draadwerk
Vuurwiel
Wanpraktyk
Wat die water onthou
Watermerke
Watervlerk
Weerlig van die ongeloof
Weerloos lewe

Bibliography

Agarwal, Apoorv, Augusto Corvalan, Jacob Jensen, and Owen Rambow. "Social Network Analysis of Alice in Wonderland." In *Workshop on Computational Linguistics for Literature*, 88–96. Montreal: Association for Computational Linguistics, 2012.

Alberich, R., J. Miro-Julia, and F. Rossello. *Marvel universe looks almost like a real social network.* 2002. http://arxiv.org/pdf/cond-mat/0202174v1.pdf (accessed March 1, 2013).

Albert, Réka, and Albert-László Barabási. "Statistical mechanics of complex networks." *Reviews of Modern Physics* 74 (2002): 47-97.

Albert, Réka, Hawoong Jeong, and Albert-László Barabási. "Error and attack tolerance of complex networks." *Nature* 406, no. 6794 (2000): 378-382.

Almack, J. C. "The influence of intelligence on the selection of associates." *School and Society* 16 (1922): 529-530.

Amaral, L.A.N., and J.M. Ottino. "Complex networks. Augmenting the framework for the study of complex systems." *European Physical Journal* 38 (2004): 147–162.

Arquilla, John, David Ronfeldt, and Michele Zanini. "Networks, Netwar, and Information-Age Terrorism." In *Strategic Appraisal: The Changing Role of Information in Warfare*, edited by Zalmay Khalilzad, John P. White and Andrew Marshall. Santa Monica: RAND, 1999.

Barabási, A.-L., and R. Albert. "Emergence of scaling in random networks." *Science* 286 (1999): 509–511.

Barabási, Albert-Láslό. *Linked.* London: Plume, 2003[2002].

Barabási, Albert-László. "Network science: Luck or reason." *Nature* 489, no. 7417 (2012): 507-508.

Barabási, Albert-László. "Scale-free networks: a decade and beyond." *Science* 325, no. 5939 (2009): 412-413.

Bar-Yam, Yaneer. *Dynamics of complex systems.* Colorado: Westview Press, 1997.

Bibliography

Bavelas, Alex. "A mathematical model for group structure." *Applied Anthropology* 7 (1948): 16-30.

Boccaletti, S., V. Latora, Y. Moreno, M. Chavez, and D.-U. Hwanga. "Complex networks: Structure and dynamics." *Physics Reports* 424 (2006): 175–308.

Boissevain, Jeremy. "Network Analysis: A Reappraisal." *Current Anthropology* 20, no. 2 (1979): 392-394.

Borgatti, Stephen P. "Identifying sets of key players in a social network." *Computational & Mathematical Organization Theory* 12, no. 1 (2006): 21-34.

Borgatti, Stephen P., Ajay Mehra, Daniel J. Brass, and Giuseppe Labianca. "Network Analysis in the Social Sciences." *Science* 323 (2009): 892-895.

Bott, H. "Observation of play activities in a nursery school." *Genetic Psychology Monographs* 4 (1928): 44-88.

Bourdieu, Pierre. "Intellectual Field and Creative Project." In *Knowledge and Control: New Directions for the Sociology of Education*, edited by M.K.D. Young. London: Collier Macmillan, 1971.

Bourdieu, Pierre. "Le champ littéraire." *Actes de la recherche en sciences sociales* 89 (1991): 4-46.

Boyd, John P., William J. Fitzgerald, Matthew C. Mahutga, and David A. Smith. "Computing continuous core/periphery structures for social relations data with MINRES/SVD." *Social Networks* 32, no. 2 (2010): 125-137.

Brownlee, Jason. "Complex Adaptive Systems." *CIS Technical Report* March (2007): 1-6.

Buchanan, Mark. *Nexus: Small worlds and the groundbreaking science of networks*. New York: W.W. Norton & Co., 2003.

Bullmore, Ed, and Olaf Sporns. "Complex brain networks: graph theoretical analysis of structural and functional systems." *Nature* 10 (2009): 186-198.

Butts, Carter T. "Social network analysis: A methodological introduction." *Asian Journal of Social Psychology* 11 (2008): 13–41.

Carley, K., M. Dombroski, M. Tsvetovat, J. Reminga, and N. Kamenva. "Destabilising Dynamic Covert Networks." In *Proceedings of the 8th International Command and Control Research and Technology Symposium*. Washington, DC: National Defence War College, 2003.

Chen, Ye-Sho, and Ferdinand F. Leimkuhler. "A relationship between Lotka's law, Bradford's law, and Zipf's law." *Journal of the American Society for Information Science* 37, no. 5 (1986): 307-314.

Chevaleva-Janovskaja, E. "Groupements spontanés d'enfants à l'age préscolaire." *Archiv es de Psychologie* 20 (1927): 219-223.

Clauset, Aaron, Cosma Rohilla Shalizi, and Mark EJ Newman. "Power-

law distributions in empirical data." *SIAM review* 51, no. 4 (2009): 661-703.
Codde, Philippe. "Polysystem Theory Revisited: A New Comparative Introduction." *Poetics Today*, no. 1 (2003): 91-126.
Committee on Network Science for Future Army Applications. *Network Science*. Washington, DC: National Academy of Sciences, 2005.
Conyon, Martin J., and Mark R. Muldoon. "The small world of corporate boards." *Journal of Business Finance & Accounting* 33, no. 9/10 (2006): 1321-1343.
Costa, Luciano da Fontoura, et al. "Analyzing and modeling real-world phenomena with complex networks: a survey of applications." *Advances in Physics* 60, no. 3 (2011): 329- 412.
De Benedictis, L., and L. Tajoli. *The World Trade Network*. University of Macerata, 2008.
De Nooy, Wouter. "Social networks and classification in literature." *Poetics* 20 (1991): 507–537.
—. "Fields and networks: Correspondence analysis and social network analysis in the framework of field theory." *Poetics* 31 (2003): 305–327.
—. *Richtingen & lichtingen. Literaire classificaties, netwerken, instituties*. Tilburg: Unpublished PhD Dissertation, University of Tilburg, 1993.
—. "The dynamics of artistic prestige." *Poetics* 30 (2002): 147–167.
De Saussure, Ferdinand. *Course of General Linguistics*. New York: McGraw-Hill, 1966.
De Wet, Karen. *Eiendoms Onbeperk: Die onvoltooide groot gesprek met D.J. Opperman in die Afrikaanse poësie*. Unpublished PhD thesis, University of Bophuthatswana, 1994.
Dempwolf, C. Scott, and L. Ward Lyles. "The Uses of Social Network Analysis in Planning: A Review of the Literature." *Journal of Planning Literature* 27, no. 1 (2012): 3-21.
Di Battista, Giuseppe, Peter Eades, Roberto Tamassia, and Ioannis G Tollis. "Algorithms for drawing graphs: an annotated bibliography." *Computational Geometry* 4, no. 5 (1994): 235-282.
DiMaggio, Paul. "On Pierre Bourdieu." *American Journal of Sociology* 84, no. 6 (1979): 1460-1474.
Donges, J.F., Y. Zou, N. Marwan, and J. Kurths. "Complex networks in climate dynamics: Comparing linear and nonlinear network construction methods." *The European Physical Journal Special Topics* 174 (2009): 157–179.
Dorogovtsev, Sergey N., and José Fernando F. Mendes. "Language as an evolving word web." *Proceedings of the Royal Society of London. Series B: Biological Sciences* 268, no. 1485 (2001): 2603-2606.
Dos Santos, Daniel A., Maria Gabriela Cuezzo, Maria Celina Reynaga, and

Eduardo Dominguez. "Towards a Dynamic Analysis of Weighted Networks in Biogeography." *Systematic Biology* 61, no. 2 (2012): 240–252.

Eades, P. "A heuristic for graph drawing." *Congressus Numerantium* 42 (1984): 149–160.

Emirbayer, Mustafa, and Jeff Goodwin. "Network analysis, culture, and the problem of agency." *American journal of sociology* 99, no. 6 (May 1994): 1411-1454.

Erdös, Paul, and Alfréd Rényi. "On the evolution of random graphs." *Publications of the Mathematical Institute of the Hungarian Academy of Sciences* 5 (1960): 17–61.

Even-Zohar, Itamar. "Polysystem Studies." *Poetics Today* 11, no. 1 (1990): 1-94.

—. "Polysystem Theory." *Poetics Today* 1, no. 1/2 (Autumn 1979): 287-310.

Everett, Martin, and Stephen P. Borgatti. "Ego network betweenness." *Social networks* 27, no. 1 (2005): 31-38.

Flandreau, M., and C. Jobst. "The Empirics of International Currencies: Network Externalities, History and Persistence." *The Economic Journal* 119, no. 537 (2009): 643-664.

Flandreau, M., and C. Jobst. "The Ties That Divide: a Network Analysis of the International Monetary System 1890-1910." *The Journal of Economic History* 65, no. 4 (2005): 977-1007.

FMS Advanced Systems Group. *Sentinel Visualizer Version 6: The New Standard for Data Visualization and Analysis*. FMS Advanced Systems Group, 2013.

Fokkema, Douwe. "The systems-theoretical perspective in literary studies: Arguments for a problem-orientated approach." *Canadian Review of Comparative Literature*, March 1997: 177-185.

Freeman, Linton C. "A set of measures of centrality based on betweenness." *Sociometry*, 1977: 35-41.

—. "The gatekeeper, pair-dependency and structural centrality." *Quality and Quantity* 14, no. 4 (1980): 585-592.

—. "Centrality in social networks conceptual clarification." *Social networks* 1, no. 3 (1979): 215-239.

—. "Some Antecedents of Social Network Analysis." *Connections* 19, no. 1 (1996): 39-42.

—. *The development of Social Network Analysis. A study in the sociology of science*. Vacouver: Empirical Press, 2004.

Fricke, Daniel, Karl Finger, and Thomas Lux. *On Assortative and Disassortative Mixing Scale-Free Networks: The Case of Interbank Credit Networks*. Kiel Working Paper No. 1830: Kiel Institute for the World Economy, 2013.

Fruchterman, Thomas M.J., and Edward M. Reingold. "Graph drawing

by force-directed placement." *Software: Practice and experience* 21, no. 11 (1991): 1129-1164.
Geyer, Felix. *Alienation, ethnicity, and postmodernism.* London: Greenwood Press, 1996.
Granovetter, M. S. "The strength of weak ties: A network theory revisited." *Sociological Theory* 1 (1983): 203-233.
—. "The Strength of Weak Ties." *American Journal of Sociology* 78, no. 6 (May 1973): 1360-1380.
Greyling, Franci. "Oor grense heen: 'n Deelnemende projek ter bevordering van skryf in ontwikkelende gemeenskappe." *Stilet* 17, no. 2 (Junie 2005): 155-177.
Guillaume, Jean-Loup, and Matthieu Latapy. "Bipartite structure of all complex networks." *Information Processing Letters* 90 (2004): 215–221.
HafnerBurton, Emilie M., Miles Kahler, and Alexander H. Montgomery. "Network Analysis for International Relations." *International Organization* 63, no. 3 (2009): 559-592.
Hagman, E. P. "The companionships of preschool children." *University of Iowa Studies in Child Welfare* 7 (1933): 10-69.
Haldane, Andrew G. "Rethinking the financial network." *Speech delivered at the Financial Student Association*, 2009: 1-41.
Haythomthwaite, Caroline. "Social Network Analysis: An Approach and Technique for the Study of Information Exchange." *LISR* 18 (1996): 323-342.
Henke, Glenn A. *How Terrorist Groups Survive: A Dynamic Network Analysis Approach to the Resilience of Terrorist Organizations.* Fort Leavenworth: School of Advanced Military Studies, 2009.
Heylighen, Francis. "Self-organization, emergence and the architecture of complexity." *Proceedings of the 1st European conference on System Science.* Paris, 1989. 23-32.
Heylighen, Francis. "The Global Superorganism: an evolutionary-cybernetic model of the emerging network society." *Social Evolution & History* 6, no. 1 (2007): 58-119.
Holliday, Emma, Clifton David Fuller, Lynn D. Wilson, and Charles R. Thomas. "Success breeds success: authorship distribution in the Red Journal, 1975-2011." *International Journal of Radiation Oncology, Biology, Physics* 85, no. 1 (2013): 23-28.
Hoppe, Bruce, and Claire Reinelt. "Social network analysis and the evaluation of leadership networks." *The Leadership Quarterly* 21, no. 4 (2010): 600-619.
Hu, Yifan. "Algorithms for visualizing large networks." *Combinatorial Scientific Computing* 5, no. 3 (2011): 180-186.
Hubbard, R. M. "A method of studying spontaneous group formation."

In *Some New Techniques for Studying Social Behavior*, edited by Dorothy Swaine Thomas, 76-85. New York: Teachers College, Columbia University, Child Development Monographs, 1929.

Jeong, H., S. P. Mason, A.-L. Barabási, and Z. N. Oltvai. "Lethality and centrality in protein networks." *Nature* 411 (2001): 41-42.

John, Philip. "De Jong, Foucault en 'n Ander Afrikaanse letterkunde: 'n Hartstogtelike mislukking." *Journal of Literary Studies* 10, no. 2 (1994): 238 — 254.

Kamada, T., and S. Kawai. "An algorithm for drawing general undirected graphs." *Information Processing Letters* 31 (1989): 7–15.

Kilcullen, David. *The accidental guerrilla. Fighting small wars in the midst of a big one*. London: Hurst & Co, 2009a.

Kitano, Hiroaki. "Computational systems biology." *Nature* 420 (2002): 206-210.

Kobourov, Stephen G. "Force-directed drawing algorithms." In *Handbook of Graph Drawing and Visualization*, edited by Roberto Tamassia, 383-408. CRC Press, 2013.

Koschade, Stuart. "A social network analysis of Jemaah Islamiyah: The applications to counterterrorism and intelligence." *Studies in Conflict & Terrorism* 29, no. 6 (2006): 559-575.

Koschade, Stuart Andrew. *The internal dynamics of terrorist cells: a social network analysis of terrorist cells in an Australian context*. Unpublished PhD thesis: Queensland University of Technology, 2007.

Krebs, Valdis E. "Mapping Networks of Terrorist Cells." *Connections* 24, no. 3 (2002): 43-52.

Kwapień, Jarosław, and Stanisław Drożdż. "Physical approach to complex systems." *Physics Reports* 515, no. 3 (2012): 115-226.

Latapy, Matthieu. "Main-memory Triangle Computations for Very Large (Sparse (Power-Law)) Graphs." *Theoretical Computer Science* 407, no. 1-3 (2008): 458-473.

Lawson, E., T. Ferris, D. Cropley, and S. Cook. *Development of a Foundation for Military Network Science*. Systems Engineering and Evaluation Centre (SEEC), University of South Australia, 2006.

Levin, Simon A. "Ecosystems and the Biosphere as Complex Adaptive Systems." *Ecosystems* 1 (1998): 431–436.

Lewin, Kurt. "Field Theory and Experiment in Social Psychology: Concepts and Methods." *American Journal of Sociology* 44, no. 6 (1939): 868-896.

—. *Field theory in social science*. New York: Harper, 1951.

Leydesdorff, Loet. "Betweenness centrality as an indicator of the interdisciplinarity of scientific journals." *Journal of the American Society for Information Science and Technology* 58, no. 9 (2007): 1303-1319.

Lotka, Afred. "The frequency distribution of scientific productivity." *Journal of the Washington Academy of Sciences* 16, no. 12 (1926): 317–324.
Luke, Douglas A., and Katherine A. Stamatakis. "Systems Science Methods in Public Health: Dynamics, Networks, and Agents." *Annual Review of Public Health* 33 (2012): 357–376.
MacRoberts, Michael H., and Barbara R. MacRoberts. "A Re-evaluation of Lotka's Law of scientific productivity." *Social Studies of Science* 12, no. 3 (1982): 443-450.
Maslov, Sergei, Kim Sneppen, and Alexei Zaliznyak. "Detection of topological patterns in complex networks: correlation profile of the internet." *Physica* 333 (2004): 529 – 540.
Mayer-Schönberger, Viktor, and Kenneth Cukier. *Big data: A revolution that will transform how we live, work and think.* London: John Murray, 2013.
Merico, Daniele, David Gfeller, and Gary D. Bader. "How to visually interpret biological data using networks." *Nature biotechnology* 27, no. 10 (2009): 921-924.
Merton, Robert K. "The Matthew Effect in science." *Science* 159, no. 3810 (1968): 56-63.
—. "The role-set: Problems in sociological theory." *British Journal of Sociology* 8 (1957): 106-120.
Midgley, G. *Systemic Intervention: Philosophy, Methodology, and Practice.* Kluwer Academic, 2000.
Milgram, Stanley. "The small world problem." *Psychology Today* 2 (1967): 60-67.
Miller, John H., and Scott E. Page. *Complex adaptive systems. An introduction to computational models of social life.* Princeton: Princeton University Press, 2007.
Mitchell, J. C. "The concept and use of social networks." In *Social networks in urban situations,* edited by J. C. Mitchell, 1-50. Manchester: Manchester University Press, 1969.
Mitchell, Melanie. "Complex systems: Network thinking." *Artificial Intelligence* 170, no. 18 (2006): 1194-1212.
Moreno, Jacob L. *Who Shall Survive?* Washington, DC: Nervous and Mental Disease Publishing Company, 1934.
Moretti, Franco. "Network theory, plot analysis." *New Left Review* 68 (2011).
Mouton, Johann. *A bibliometric analysis of the state of research at UFS.* Stellenbosch: Unpublished Report, 2013.
Nadel, S. F. *The Theory of Social Structure.* Glencoe: Free Press, 1957.
Nemeth, Roger, and David A. Smith. "International Trade and World-System Structure: A Multiple Network Analysis." *Review* 8 (1985): 517-560.

Newman, M. E. J. "The Structure and Function of Complex Networks." *SIAM Review* 45, no. 2 (2003): 167–256.
—. "Power laws, Pareto distributions and Zipf's law." *Contemporary physics* 46, no. 5 (2005): 323-351.
Newman, M. E. J., and M. Girvan. "Finding evaluating community structure in networks." *Physical review* 69, no. 2 (2004).
O'Boyle, Ernest, and Herman Aguinis. "The Best and the Rest: Revisiting the Norm of Normality of Individual Performance." *Personnel Psychology* 65 (2012): 79–119.
Ottino, Julio M. "New Tools, New Outlooks, New Opportunities." *AIChE Journal* 51, no. 7 (2005): 1840-1845.
Pareto, V. *Le cours d'economie politique.* London: Macmillan, 1897.
Petraeus, David. *The U.S. Army and Marine Corps Counterinsurgency Field Manual.* Washington: Department of the Army and Department of the Navy, 2006.
Pool, Ithiel de Sola, and Manfred Kochen. "Contacts and influence." *Social networks* 1, no. 1 (1979): 5-51.
Prell, Christina. *Social Network Analysis. History, theory and methodology.* London: Sage, 2012.
Prigogine, Ilya. *The end of certainty. Time, chaos, and the new laws of nature.* New York: The Free Press, 1997.
—. "Time, structure, and fluctuations." *Science* 201, no. 4358 (1978): 777-785.
Ressler, Steve. "Social Network Analysis as an Approach to Combat Terrorism: Past, Present, and Future Research." *Homeland Security Affairs* 2, no. 2 (2006): 1-10.
Rodriguez, Jose A. *The March 11th Terrorist Network: In its weakness lies its strength.* Los Angeles: XXV International Sunbelt Conference, 2005.
Rowlands, Ian. "Emerald authorship data, Lotka's law and research productivity." *Aslib Proceedings* 57, no. 1 (2005): 5-10.
Rydberg-Cox, Jeff. "Social networks and the language of greek tragedy." *Journal of the Chicago Colloquium on Digital Humanities and Computer Science* 1, no. 3 (2011): 1-11.
Sack, Alexander Graham. *Bleak house and weak social networks.* Unpublished PhD Thesis: Columbia University, 2006.
Schmidt, Siegfried J. "A systems-orientated approach to literary studies." *Canadian Review of Comparative Literature,* March 1997: 119-136.
Scott, John. *What is Social Network Analysis?* London: Bloomsbury Academic, 2012.
Seeman, Melvin. "On the meaning of alienation." *American Sociological Review* 24, no. 6 (1959): 783-791.
Senekal, Burgert A. *'n Bespreking van die Afrikaanse poësienetwerk sedert*

2000. 2013d. http://www.litnet.co.za/Article/n-bespreking-van-die-afrikaanse-posienetwerk-sedert-2000 (accessed May 10, 2013).
—. "'n Netwerkontleding van die Afrikaanse poësienetwerk vanaf 2000 tot 2012." *Stilet*, 2013a: 99-124.
—. "'n Inligtingstegnologie-gesentreerde gebruikerskoppelvlak vir navorsingsdoeleindes binne die geesteswetenskappe met spesifieke verwysing na die Afrikaanse letterkunde." *LitNet Akademies* 9, no. 2 (2012a): 468-499.
—. "'n Netwerkontleding van karakterverhoudinge in Etienne van Heerden se Toorberg." *Literator* 34, no. 2 (2013b): 1-9.
—. "'n Ontleding van Hertzogpryswenners se uitgeweryprofiele in terme van die Afrikaanse literêre netwerk en met behulp van Sosiale-netwerk-analise (SNA)." *LitNet Akademies* 10, no. 3 (2013e).
—. "Die Afrikaanse literêre sisteem: 'n Eksperimentele benadering met behulp van Sosiale-netwerk-analise (SNA)." *LitNet Akademies* 9, no. 3 (December 2012b): 614-638.
—. "Die gebruik van die netwerkteorie binne 'n sisteemteoretiese benadering tot die Afrikaanse letterkunde: 'n Teorie-oorsig." *Tydskrif vir Geesteswetenskappe* 53, no. 4 (2013c).
—. "'n Verwysingsanalise van akademiese artikels binne die Afrikaanse letterkunde." *LitNet Akademies*, 2014: Forthcoming.
—. "The Mirror and the Universe in Christine Brooke-Rose's Life, End of." *Textures* 21 (2007): 23-39.
Senekal, J. H. *Literatuuropvattings: 'wese' en 'waarhede' van 'n nuwe literêre teorie*. Bloemfontein: University of the Free State, 1987.
—. *'n Beskrywing van die Afrikaanse literatuursisteem*. Unpublished report by the RGN, 1986.
Serrat, Olivier. *Social Network Analysis*. Washington, DC: Asian Development Bank, 2010.
Shavit, Zohar. "Canonicity and Literary Institutions." In *Empirical Studies of Literature*, edited by Elrud Ibsch, 231-238. Amsterdam: Rodopi, 1991.
Shklovsky, Viktor. "Art as technique." In *Literary theory: An anthology*, edited by Julie Rivkin and Michael Ryan. Oxford: Blackwell, 2004.
Simmel, George. *Conflict and the web of group affilliations*. Translated by Kurt H. Wolff. New York: Free press, 1922.
Smith, David A., and Douglas R. White. "Structure and Dynamics of the Global Economy: Network Analysis of International Trade1965-1980." *Social Forces* 70, no. 4 (1992): 857-893.
Snyder, David, and Edward Kick. "Structural Position in the World System and Economic Growth: A Multiple Network Analysis of Transnational interactions." *American Journal of Sociology* 84 (1979): 1096-112.

Solé, Ricard V., Bernat Corominas-Murtra, Sergi Valverde, and Luc Steels. "Language networks: Their structure, function, and evolution." *Complexity* 15, no. 6 (2010): 20-26.

Sparrow, M.K. "The application of network analysis to criminal intelligence: An assessment of the prospects." *Social Networks* 13 (1991): 251-274.

Steiber, Steven. "The World System and World Trade: An Empirical Explanation of Conceptual Conflicts." *The Sociological Quarterly* 20 (1979): 23-36.

Strogatz, Steven. *Sync. The emerging science of spontaneous order.* London: Penguin, 2004[2003].

Sun, Shiwei, Lunjiang Ling, Nan Zhang, Guojie Li, and Runsheng Chen. "Topological structure analysis of the protein-protein interaction network in budding yeast." *Nucleic Acids Research* 31, no. 9 (2003): 2443-2450.

Suderman, Matthew, and Michael Hallett. "Tools for visually exploring biological networks." *Bioinformatics* 23, no. 20 (2007): 2651-2659.

Tichy, Noel M., Michael L. Tushman, and Charles Fombrun. "Social Network Analysis for Organizations." *The Academy of Management Review* 4, no. 4 (1979): 507-519.

Van Coller, H. P. "Literatuur in die marge: Die plek van die middelmootliteratuur." *LitNet Akademies* 8, no. 2 (2011): 66-89.

—. "Antjie Krog se vertaling van Henk van Woerden se roman Een mond vol glas." *Literator* 23, no. 2 (August 2002): 129-163.

Van Coller, H. P., and B. J. Odendaal. "Die verhouding tussen die Afrikaanse en Nederlandse literêre sisteme: deel 1: oorwegings vir'n beskrywende model." *Stilet* 11, no. 3 (2005): 1-17.

—. "Die meer ''beskeie'' opsies van 'n ''buitestander'': M. Nienaber-Luitingh in die Afrikaanse literêre sisteem." *LitNet Akademies* 5, no. 3 (December 2008): 33-50.

—. "Kleur kom nooit alleen nie (Antjie Krog) en Die burg van hertog Bloubaard (H.J. Pieterse): 'n poëtikale beskouing (Deel 1)." *Stilet* 15, no. 1 (March 2003): 16-35.

Van Gorp, Hendrik. "Introduction: The study of literature and culture - Systems and fields." *Canadian Review of Comparative Literature*, March 1997: 1-5.

Van Rees, Kees, and Gillis J. Dorleijn. "Het Nederlandse literaire veld 1800-2000." In *De produktie van literatuur. Het literaire veld in Nederland 1800-2000*, edited by Gillis J. Dorleijn and Kees Van Rees, 15-38. Nijmegen: Vantilt, 2006.

Van Rees, Kees, Susanne Janssen, and Marc Verboord. "Classificatie in het culturele en literaire veld 1975-2000. Diversificatie en nivellering van

grenzen tussen culturele genres." In *De produktie van literatuur. Het literaire veld in Nederland 1800-2000*, edited by Gillis J. Dorleijn and Kees Van Rees, 239-284. Nijmegen: Vantilt, 2006.
Venter, Cristél. "'n Sisteemteoretiese Perspektief op die Vertaling van Suid-Afrikaanse Literatuur in Nederlands." Unpublished PhD thesis: University of the Free State, 2002.
Venter, Rudi. *Die materiële produksie van Afrikaanse fiksie (1990-2005): 'n Empiriese ondersoek na die produksieprofiel en uitgeweryprofiel binne die uitgeesisteem.* Unpublished PhD thesis: University of Pretoria, 2006.
Verboord, M. "Classification of authors by literary prestige." *Poetics*, 2003: 259–81.
Verboord, Marc, Susanne Janssen, and Kees Van Rees. "Indicatoren voor classificatie in het culturele en literaire veld." In *De produktie van literatuur. Het literaire veld in Nederland 1800-2000*, edited by Gillis J. Dorleijn and Kees Van Rees, 285-310. Nijmegen: Vantilt, 2006.
Vilar, J. M. G., and J. M. Rubi. "Thermodynamics 'beyond' Local Equilibrium." *Proceedings of the National Academy of Sciences of the United States of America* 98, no. 20 (September 2001): 11081-11084.
Viljoen, Hein M. *Die Suid-Afrikaanse romansisteem - 'n vergelykende studie.* Unpublished PhD thesis: University of Potchefstroom, 1986.
—. "Die literêre sisteem van Dertig." *Literator* 5, no. 1 (1984): 65-74.
Von Bertalanffy, Ludwig. *General systems theory: Foundations, development, applications.* New York: George Braziller, 1968.
Vorster, Charl. *General Systems Theory and psychotherapy: beyond post-modernism.* Riviera: Satori, 2003.
Wang, Xiao Fan. "Complex Networks: Typology, dynamics and synchronization." *International Journal of Bifurcation and Chaos*, 12, no. 5 (2002): 885–916.
Watts, Duncan J., and S. H. Strogatz. "Collective dynamics of 'small-world' networks." *Nature* 393, no. 6684 (1998): 409-410.
Watts, Duncan J. *Six Degrees. The Science of a Connected Age.* London: Vintage, 2004[2003].
—. *Everything is obvious. Once you know the answer.* London: Atlantic, 2011.
—. *Small Worlds: The dynamics of networks between order and randomness.* Princeton: Princeton University Press, 1999.
Watts, Duncan J., and Steve Hasker. "Marketing in an unpredictable world." *Harvard Business Review* 84, no. 9 (2006): 25-30.
Weideman, Albert. *A framework for the study of linguistics.* Pretoria: Van Schaik, 2011.
Wellman, Barry. "The school child's choice of companions." *Journal of Educational Research* 14 (1926): 126-132.

—. "Network Analysis: Some Basic Principles." *Sociological Theory*, 1 (1983): 155-200.

Wilden, Anthony. *System and structure: essays in communication and exchange*. New York: Tavistock, 1980.

Zhu, Bin, Stephanie Watts, and Hsinchun Chen. "Visualizing social network concepts." *Decision Support Systems* 49, no. 2 (2010): 151-161.

Notes

1 Own translation. The original reads, "Dit is vernuwend ten opsigte van 'n anderste kyk na die Afrikaanse poësiesisteem. Die artikelskrywer moet geluk gewens word hiermee dat hy/sy vernuwend kyk na die Afrikaanse literêre veld en daardeur 'n bydrae lewer tot die gesprek rondom die Afrikaanse poësie."

2 Own translation. The original reads, "'n Duifie wat 90 keer koer in 'n eikelaning het seker dus meer graadsentraliteit as 'n leeu wat een keer in dieselfde laning brul. Maar wie het die grootste uitwerking/ meeste invloed? In die literêre wêreld is dit byvoorbeeld algemeen bekend dat 'n uitgewery soos Protea werk van mindere digters publiseer, 'n feit wat ook weerspieël word deur die beperkte aantal pryse wat die skrywers wat by Protea publiseer, inpalm. Tog is dit, soos in die artikel aangedui, 'n feit dat Protea die meeste digbundels publiseer. Die digbundels wat Protea publiseer, verkeer nietemin op die periferie weens die mindere gehalte van die poësie."

3 In following Viljoen (1986, 3), Lawson, Ferris, Cropley and Cook (2006, 9), and Sentinel Visualizer, I use the term *entity* throughout this book to denote elements, nodes, actors, organizations, role players, phenomena etc. that are part of the system.

4 Search terms are provided in brackets throughout this book.

5 The complete integration of field theory with polysystem theory is however problematic; see Codde (2003) and Van Rees and Dorleijn (2006, 23). Although field theory and polysystem theory are highly similar, they are not identical. Nevertheless, they are often treated as identical, and Van Coller (2011, 69) for instance uses the terms *literary system* and *literary field* as synonyms. Also note that Bourdieu rejected the use of network analysis, *but* "several researchers have used social network analysis in their efforts to apply and test Bourdieu's field theory" (W. De Nooy 2003, 306). De Nooy discusses the application of SNA to Bourdieu's theory in detail; because Bourdieu's field

150   Notes

theory is used in this book in a supplementary capacity (supplemental to systems theory), the small differences between these approaches are not dealt with here.

6   Translated from the original, which reads, "Literatuur word vandag vrywel algemeen as sisteem beskou, nie as 'n versameling boeke/tekste/taalbousels nie".

7   Note however that De Nooy does not discuss the literary system as a *complex* network, but rather focuses on the micro-level application of network theory, i.e. SNA.

8   Translated from the original: "Die inherente gebrek aan sisteemdenke is die onmoontlikheid van verifikasie omdat dit 'n interpretatiewe konstruksie is".

9   Translated from the original, "'n Literatuurwetenskap wat die literatuursisteem/sisteme ontleed, en nie vir hom 'n 'spesiale status en andersheid' opeis nie, wat nie deur poëtikas en attitudes gerig word nie maar deurwetenskapsfilosofiese oorwegings, kan nagaan hoe 'n sisteem daar uitsien, hoe dit funksioneer, of die gemeenskap gelukkig is daarmee. Verder kan dit die interne relasies beskryf tussen literatuurproduksie, literatuurverspreiding, literatuurresepsie en literatuurverwerking of –verbruik".

10 Translated from the original, "Wanneer literatuur nie as die geringe getal boeke en skrywersop die E-vlak opgevat word nie, maar as handelinge in 'nliterêre kommunikasiesisteem wat oor die hele spektrum strek,kan 'n mens 'n volediger beeld kry van hoe die literatuursisteemsaamgestel en georganiseer word. Dit is waarom dit hier gaan".

11 Quoted in Amaral and Ottino (2004, 151).

12 Hennings contributed to *Who shall survive*, but was not credited as a co-author.

13 Bourdieu (1991, 4) defines the cultural field as, "social spaces where the agents who contribute to the productionof cultural works are situated" (translation Codde 2003, 107). In terms of the cultural field, the works of Pierre Bourdieu, who was "Inspired, at least in part, by the vector psychology of Kurt Lewin" (DiMaggio 1979, 1462), are more familiar than Kurt Lewin's insights, but are conceptually highly similar. Bourdieu (1971, 161) for instance recognizes the importance of emergence and the resulting impossibility of reducing the study of a complex system to its constituent parts (although he does not use this terminology): "The intellectual field, [...] cannot be reduced to a simple aggregate of isolated agents or to the sum of elements merely juxtaposed."

14 Freeman (1980, 586) notes that Bavelas's "intuition was not embodied in a formally defined measure."
15 Mitchell (1969) describes the field of SNA by the end of the 1960s.
16 SNA was however an improvement over existing link analysis, not an entirely new concept. During WWII, the Intelligence Community (IC) developed "traffic analysis" (also known as *communication link analysis*), as Ressler (2006, 6)explains, "This technique consists of the study of the external characteristics of communication in order to get information about the organization of the communication system. It is not concerned with the content of phone calls, but is interested in who calls whom and the network members, messengers, and gatekeepers. Traffic analysis was used by the British MI5 internal security service to combat the IRA in the 1980s and 1990s and continues to be used across the world by law-enforcement agencies including the U.S. Defense Intelligence Agency (DIA) Office of National Drug Control Policy."
17 Translated from the original, "Kultuur is 'n web, nie 'n stukkie drukwerk in isolasie nie".
18 Systems theory and cybernetics are related through particularly Gregory Bateson, see e.g. Vorster (2003) and Wilden (1980).
19 See in this respect Viljoen's (1986, 6) distinction between deterministic and stochastic systems.
20 Translated from the original, which reads, "'n Boek wat nie gerensenseer word nie, en nie deur een van die erkende, gekeurde, resensente gerensenseer word nie, kan moeilik as letterkunde beskou word, of in letterkundegeskiedenisse opgeneem word."
21 Translated from the original, which reads, "dit pos die boek na die geskiedenis, na die onverganklike en soos vroeër geglo is: die monumente-komitees".See also Van Rees, Janssen and Verboord (2006, 268).
22 Translated from the original: "Op langere termijn behelst het product van een uitgeverij, haar fonds, behalve economische ook symbolische waarde, die afstraalt op nieuwkommers. Het uitgevershuis mag prestigious heten, omdat het gerenommeerde auteurs in zijn fonds telt. Wordt het manuscript van een onbekende debutant uitgegeven door een dergelijk toonaangevend huis, dan straalt dat aanzien af op deze debutant".
23 Senekal (1987, 177) writes, "Ditis algemeen bekend dat koerante en tydskrifte die resensie-eksemplare net aan sekere persone stuur en slegs daardie persone se resensies aanvaar" [It is well known that newspapers and magazines send review copies only to certain persons and only those people's reviews are accepted.]

Notes

24 Translated from the original: "Hierdie kanon van werke wat 'n spesiale status in die samelewing geniet staan egter ook nie 'onbeweeglik' nie. Dit bevat 'n aantal 'monumente', maar ditbevat ook werke wat in- en uitgeskuif word volgens persoonlikesiening".

25 Translated from the original, "Die resensent of kritikus, die literatuurwetenskaplike, die uitgewer of handelaar, die onderwyser - hulle almal bepaal wat literatuur is en wat nie. Dit wil sê: sosiale handelinge beslis oor en rig die sisteem literatuur, nie (net) 'literêre waarde' nie".

26 Translated from the original: "Het culturele veld ligt ingebed in de samenleving, opgevat als het geheel van onderling afhanklijke sferen: naast de culturele, met name de politieke, de economische en de sociale sfeer. Inbedding betekent dat de politieke beslissingen en sosiaal-economische faktoren van invloed zijn op wat er in het culturele veld gebeurt. Tegelijkerijd echter oefent ook cultuur zelf [...] invloed uit op de samenleving".

27 Translated from the original, "Selfs Afrikaanse literêre handelinge bestaan nie in isolasie nie, maar is ten nouste verweef met die internasionale wêreld en sy denke - waarmee dit inderdaad selfs elektronies verbind is. Dit is vandag baie duideliker só as in vorige dekades en toe reeds, van die begin van die Afrikaanse literatuur af, was daar baie sterk import van ander literature na Afrikaans, uit sowel Westerse as uit Afrikatradisies".

28 One sees a continuation of this innovation in novels such as Etienne van Heerden's *Toorberg* and Marlene van Niekerk's *Agaat*, see e.g. Senekal (2013b).

29 Because Visualizer cannot calculate average path length and other macrolevel features of complex networks, these were calculated using Gephi.

30 For the sake of consistency, this chapter uses the same Fruchterman Reingold force-directed layout found in Gephi to visualize all example networks. Later chapters visualize networks using Sentinel Visualizer.

31 The bell curve is often used in teaching, where the 'ideal' test follows the bell curve distribution of student marks, with most student marks falling around the average, few students scoring high marks, and few scoring exceptionally low marks. O'Boyle and Aguinis (2012) however show that individual performance does not follow the Gaussian distribution, but rather the Paretian (power law) distribution.

32 Newman (2005, 327) writes that Pareto's Law and Zipf's Law are "effectively synonymous" with the term "power-law distribution."

33 Barabási (2012, 507). Newman (2005, 348) also notes the highly similar Yule process, "a rich-get-richer mechanism in which the most populous cities or best-selling books get more inhabitants or sales in proportion to the number they already have."
34 Holliday et al. (2013, 24) also write, "The wide applicability of this bibliometric phenomenon suggests that it may also provide insight into other competitive human activities."
35 The network has been decluttered for clarification purposes.
36 Translated from the original, "Netwerkontledings soos hierdie kan 'n belangrike stap wees daartoe dat die bestudering van die literêre sisteem meer wetenskaplik gedoen word. Maar dit het ook breër implikasies: word 'n kongres gereël oor marginaliteit in die poësie, hoe word die digters gekies wat as marginaal bestempel word? Word 'n samestelling van Afrikaanse poësie gepubliseer, of 'n boek soos Perspektief en profiel, hoe word besluit watter digters ingesluit word en watter nie? Word 'n spesiale uitgawe van 'n joernaal oor die Afrikaanse poësie beplan, wie behoort die redakteur te wees? Die netwerkteorie verskaf 'n wetenskaplike basis om sulke besluite te neem".

www.ingramcontent.com/pod-product-compliance
Lightning Source LLC
Chambersburg PA
CBHW031226170426
43191CB00030B/231